ARCHITECTURE IN CONTEXT
fitting new buildings with old

BRENT C. BROLIN

VNR VAN NOSTRAND REINHOLD COMPANY
New York Cincinnati Toronto London Melbourne

To Jeannie

Printed in the United States of America.
Designed by Loudan Enterprise.

Published by Van Nostrand Reinhold Company
A division of Litton Educational Publishing, Inc.
135 West 50th Street, New York, NY 10020, U.S.A.

Van Nostrand Reinhold Limited
1410 Birchmount Road
Scarborough, Ontario MlP 2E7, Canada

Van Nostrand Reinhold Australia Pty. Ltd.
17 Queen Street
Mitcham, Victoria 3132, Australia

Van Nostrand Reinhold Company Limited
Molly Millars Lane
Wokingham, Berkshire, England

16 15 14 13 12 11 10 9 8 7 6 5 4 3 2 1

Library of Congress Cataloging in Publication Data

Brolin, Brent C
    Architecture in context.

    Includes index.
    1. Architecture—Environmental aspects. 2. Archi-
tecture and history.   I. Title.
NA2542.35.B76   720′.1   79–15239
ISBN 0–442–20733–6

Acknowledgments

This book follows the path laid by certain planning boards, preservation groups, and a few architects, whose overriding concern for visual continuity in our architectural surroundings has persisted in spite of the indifference of main-line modern architects. I am indebted to these people for having laid a solid groundwork for *Architecture in Context*. In trying to codify design criteria for fitting new architecture with old they have acknowledged that the richest architectural experience must include references to both past and present.

There are many people whom I would like to thank for assisting me in my research for this book; among them are those who responded to magazine queries requesting examples of buildings which they felt fit well in their surroundings. I extend special thanks to Michael Leventhal and others at the National Trust for Historic Preservation, in Washington, D.C., who generously lent me their time and facilities.

Thanks also to Ed Polonsky whose many postcards from his far-flung travels kept me informed about the world-wide nature of the problem of fitting new architecture with old.

Also, my appreciation to Elizabeth Kline and John Zeisel whose expert advice guided the "Handbook" section. And to Jeannie, Hans, Eva, Susan, Eric, and many other friends who offered valuable advice on portions of the manuscript and kept their eyes open for examples which might be useful in the book. In a sense this book is very much a joint effort.

Finally, my sincere respect and appreciation to my dear friend Angus Macdonald, whose "alternative" photomontage sketches show that there *are* ways to make visual connections if we address our skills to finding them.

The research, photography, and writing of this book would not have been possible without a generous grant from the National Endowment for the Arts.

Contents

Preface

In preparing *Architecture in Context* I placed queries both in professional and general-interest publications asking for examples of buildings which demonstrated a sympathetic relationship to their architectural surroundings. I visited and photographed as many of these as I thought looked promising. There are no examples in this book which I have not seen. Because of the limitations of time and money, I have undoubtedly missed many good examples with which the reader may be familiar.

I also made the decision not to include unfinished or unbuilt projects, such as the appealing houses designed by Charles Moore for Williamsburg, Virginia, because of my conviction that the only proper test of how well a building relates to its context is to see it in place.

My historical examples come mainly from Europe because there are more layers of history there; the contemporary ones generally come from the United States. Geographical location should actually have little bearing on the subject, however, because the examples have been selected to represent specific instances of the application of general visual principles. Yet, while these are general principles, it is essential to recognize that each individual site will demand special attention. What is successful in one context may not be appropriate in another which appears similar. There are too many variables to permit the simple transference of a solution from one site to another, or to assume that a good fit will be guaranteed if only designers will follow a set of rigid design criteria, or even design priorities. As we will see later, some buildings meet many of these criteria and still do not fit well, while others ignore even the important ones and yet succeed.

1

Introduction

There are a variety of ways to design a new building so that it is sympathetic to its architectural context. On the one hand one may literally copy architectural elements from the surroundings; on the other, one may use totally new forms to evoke, perhaps even to enhance, the visual flavor of existing buildings. The thesis of *Architecture in Context* is that either of these approaches, or anything in-between, is satisfactory as long as it is skillfully done. My eye is offended neither by fake styles nor by radical innovations as long as a strong and eloquent visual relationship has been established.

Architecture in Context is concerned with questions of architectural style and with the difficulties involved in establishing a family resemblance between buildings of different eras and styles which stand side by side. Such sympathy has not been a primary concern of architects in the past half-century. We have been taught to "contrast" new and old rather than to make them visually compatible. Contemporary architects who would not be caught dead wearing polka-dot ties with striped shirts and checkered suits think nothing of dotting our cities with the architectural equivalents of such surprising sartorial combinations.

Architecture in Context has a limited scope. Its examples come only from Europe and America. In each case it assumes that the designer has chosen to respect the context into which his building has been placed unless otherwise discussed in the text. It looks *only* at the visual problems which designers face when trying to fit new buildings with old. It does not try to measure the absolute beauty of these designs, their success in performing the assigned functions or their relationship to nature. The book recognizes, finally, that not all buildings need to or should fit harmoniously with their neighbors. There are some instances where, for aesthetic or symbolic reasons, contrast is appropriate. These will be discussed in Appendix A.

I have also made the assumption that it is possible to fit virtually any architectural program requirement behind a facade of any style, including a modern one. In *Complexity and Contradiction in Architecture* (1966) Robert Venturi showed that disguising interior functions with exterior forms was a common occurrence in pre-modernist architecture. (I use the term "modernist" to refer to the schools of twentieth century design which grew out of the International Style.) The Renaissance palazzo had uniform fenestration masking rooms with disparate uses. Early modern buildings enthusiastically used factory forms and detailing for office buildings, homes, theaters, and so on. It is implicit in my assumption that no virtue or higher morality is served by expressing interior uses "honestly" on the exterior. This is one moral preoccupation of modernism which should be less important than the visual relationship between the building's exterior and its architectural context.

This is not to say that one cannot have both a good relationship to the context and a close correlation between plan and exterior. Having different layers of meaning has never precluded a sympathetic contextual relationship. But this perhaps over-intellectualized concern has too long outweighed, in my opinion, concern for the context as a whole.

The aim of *Architecture in Context* is to learn what we can about making coherent, sympathetic visual relationships between buildings. It does not make general criticism of buildings, nor does it catalog facts about their architectural history. Few if any of the examples in this book are completely successful at fitting in, although readers' views will surely vary. In preparing the manuscript I have found that the opinion of colleagues whom I respect is often totally at odds with mine, and I assume that the reactions of readers will be at least as varied.

In some cases I have suggested alternatives to existing designs. Counter to modernist practice, we wanted these to blend quietly into their surroundings. If it is at all possible, we ask readers to view these alternatives with a fresh mind and eye, as though the residue of sixty years of modernism had evaporated from our consciousness. With our circumscribed interest in mind, try not to judge these alternatives on their intrinsic worth as architectural compositions, or as examples of styles long out of fashion in professional circles, but on how well they succeed or fail in meeting our goal: to establish a sympathetic connection to their neighbors.

The difficulty in agreeing on which relationships are successful, and which are not, became clear to me at a 1977 conference on fitting new architecture with old that was sponsored by the National Trust for Historic Preservation. Slides were shown contrasting different pairs of buildings; one supposedly fit into its context well while the other did not. The problem was that the audience often could not agree on which building fit and which did not. My analyses of the examples in this book are, of course, subjective. My aim is to stimulate discussion of the problems and to cultivate our visual awareness.

The longer one studies the question of fitting new architecture with old, however, the more demanding one becomes. I am sure that this is true of any specialization, but it became particularly apparent to me recently when I was invited, with another architect, to speak at an architecture school on the subject of fitting new with old. I gave my viewpoint in the keynote speech and the architect followed with illustrations of his work which he felt successfully harmonized with their respective contexts.

When both presentations were over, the conference organizer drew me aside to say that, had she seen the architect's slides a year ago, when she first began thinking about the subject, she would have been convinced that they were successful. But after having studied the problems for some time and refined her perceptions, she simply was not convinced. As the eye becomes attuned it becomes more and more demanding.

It is unlikely, therefore, that the casual reader will profit from merely glancing through this book. It will only confirm his or her prejudices. The proposition is complicated and needs peaceful, leisurely visual study. In the end, I hope that patient readers will sense a change in their criteria for judging the relationship between new architecture and old.

How We Arrived at our Present Attitude

Most contemporary buildings do not fit sympathetically into traditional, non-modern surroundings, no matter what the period. Some even ignore their contexts intentionally. Fitting *modern* architecture into a *modern* context, on the other hand, has almost always been a simpler matter. This does not mean that contemporary buildings which ignore their non-modern contexts are necessarily ugly, or that in some cases they are not more important than the contexts they ignore. But it does show the fundamentally egotistical and anti-social character of the Movement in this regard.

A well-known architecture critic, referring to a proposed design to be inserted into a row of Greek Revival townhouses in Greenwich Village, recently wrote that a building which blends too well with its surroundings was a "soft and [creatively] weak" solution. (See page 72) The correct, and presumably more virile, creative solution is the uncompromising *personal architectural statement*, the strength of which seems best measured in our times by how violently it offends its surroundings. If a design does not stand out from its neighbors, most believers in modern architecture seem to feel it has failed: it is neither original nor creative.

Superficially this indifference—indeed hostility —to harmonious continuity comes from the modernists' violent denunciation of derivative architectural forms. The modernist architectural code of ethics maintained that history was irrelevant, that our age was unique and therefore our architecture must be cut off from the past. Just a few short decades ago modernists argued that everyone in the world, their tastes freed by the Movement, would soon want to live in the same kind of houses, in the same kind of modern cities, all of which would reflect the spirit of *our* times. (While the "times" were always "ours," the decision as to which forms characterized them was always "theirs," the architectural elite.) Because of this overwhelming belief several generations of architects have felt little need to accommodate their work to the older, theoretically obsolete architecture around it. They have been designing their buildings as if they were going to exist in a visual vacuum.

The devastating consequences of this attitude assault us in every major city of the world. Ironically, the roots of modernism are nearly two hundred years old; they come directly from the prevailing 18th- and 19th-century Romantic's view of the artist.

By the early part of the last century the mass-productive capacities of the Industrial Revolution had fostered the first mass-market for all kinds of goods, including Art. The new market was attuned to the middle class because they had the most money with which to buy these goods. If a commodity would not sell, whether it was a line of hats or a painting, merchants were generally not interested in it.

Artists of all kinds were pressured to conform to the wishes of the new tastemakers and the Romantics rebelled against this as a vulgarization of their Art. Part of their rebellion took the form of a subtle change in the definition of Art which has come down to us today relatively unchanged. The Romantics placed a unique emphasis on *originality* and *creativity*. In *Aesthetics and Art Theory*, Harold Osborn writes, *"For the first time in history, apart from some early anticipations in Chinese art theory, originality came to be accepted as a necessary quality of great art and of the artist."* (Page 195, my emphasis.) Originality had been one possible measure of artistic success in the past, but never *the* measure, as it became in certain circles in the 19th century and remains today, to the detriment of the visual continuity of our communities. If you wanted to be thought of as a serious artist, in their terms, you had to flout the popular idea of beauty and create your own. You had to make your own *personal statement*; otherwise you were a mere copier, an artistic hack.

Ultimately the emphasis on genius and originality replaced the previous stress on excellence of execution. Renaissance artists had not wrung their hands, worrying that the Madonna and Child they were painting had already been painted thousands of times before. They counted on the brilliance of their execution *within the constraints of the given context*. By the second part of the 19th century even traditional subject matter had become suspect among the avant-garde and we find artists like Millet painting monumental works about peasants, something which would have been unheard of before.

By the mid-19th century some of these Romantic ideas had infiltrated the other visual arts, helping to foster a reform movement which began in

England. One of its aims was to raise the level of middle class taste. The Arts and Crafts Movement, officially founded in 1875 and led by William Morris, is the best-known manifestation of this artistic pedagogy. By the 1890s, however, it had become evident that the reformers had failed. Middle class taste would not be "elevated," at least not enough to satisfy the reformers.

This preoccupation with originality—in terms of expressing the artist's innermost feelings—and the "shock the bourgeoisie" sentiment together helped to bring about a 180° reversal of the definition of architectural beauty. By the beginning of our century the factory had already become an object of admiration and the factory owner's eclectic villa the butt of aesthetic ridicule. The Beast had become beautiful and Beauty had become the Beast. The Modern Movement in architecture had begun.

Wrought-iron bedstead and canopy by Charles Eastlake, an influential member of the reform movement in design. "Good" design, ca. 1878.

Belgian bedstead in the Italian style, exhibited at the Crystal Palace, London, 1851. Considered "bad" design by the reformers.

The "factory-owner's house."

706. J. P. Hale, Piano Manufactory, Tenth Ave. and Thirty-fifth St., New York, N.Y. c. 1884. [1]

The factory-owner's factory.

Historians have asserted that this aesthetic "flip-flop" took place because architects once again allowed the light of reason and aesthetic morality to govern their work. But exactly the same rational, moral and functional/economic rhetoric that eventually carried the day for modernism had been used to justify the 19th century Gothic Revival. The change is better described as an angry reaction to what artists considered corrupt bourgeois values. It was led by men like Emile Zola, Oscar Wilde, George Bernard Shaw and Clive Bell, whose sensibilities, as Jacques Barzun put it, were exasperated. Until that time artists had been trying to educate the middle classes; from then on they were on the attack.

The majority of modernist buildings erected before World War I were industrial buildings. This was largely because the mechanistic style was thought to be best suited to industry; few clients

Ornamental details such as this Gothic Revival pinnacle on St. Patrick's Cathedral, New York City, were commonly justified as functional and economic, precisely the same arguments that would be used a few decades later to justify the naked forms of modernism. (James Renwick, 1880–1884.)

Apartment house, by Mies van der Rohe, Weissenhof Housing Settlement, Stuttgart, Germany, 1927.

were bold enough to risk this new architectural fashion in surroundings meant more for human beings than machines.

By the mid-1920s modernism was beginning to be accepted outside the profession. But it was thought of as only one more choice in an already long list of possibilities. Specifically, it was a style that was particularly suited to commercial buildings and worker's housing. Though it comes as a surprise to lay people, modernists never thought of their architecture as a "style," like Louis XIV or Italian Renaissance. They considered it the inevitable, logical result of economic and functional necessity; the rational, immutable product of our times.

Their indifference to how this new architecture affected its surroundings grew naturally from their elitist viewpoint. Buttressed by the new gospel of functionalism, it seemed irrelevant and even a bit sacrilegious for modernists to question whether their new architecture fit into the newly anachronistic leavings of earlier builders. Therefore, few architects did. Even fewer do today.

To the enthusiastic modernist, indeed, it was essential that a building stand out from its neighbors, as a symbol of the future. This visual incongruity was literally *not seen* as a problem. Modernists looked beyond these visual facts to an ideal future when older buildings would no longer crowd in on their dreams. They, and those who shared their reveries, ignored the visually inadequate past and present in their quest for a grander future.

A modern mish-mash, Harvard University.

A New Way of Seeing

For better or worse, the economic and social evolution of our cities has failed to follow the modernists' predictions and modernist and traditional architecture continue to exist awkwardly side by side. As the radiance of their vision dimmed over the decades, our eyes grew accustomed to the lesser light and we began to see the relationship of new and old differently; contrasts between traditional styles and the style of "progress" that once seemed acceptable now seem harsh and insensitive.

In recent years the lay public has shown increasing signs of rebellion. Examples of community groups banding together to stave off yet another insensitive architectural intrusion appear regularly. Recent court rulings on the inappropriateness of proposed buildings to their contexts have made it apparent that we will hear more rather than less about this in the future. Why is our perception changing? Why do we now "see" these buildings differently in their surroundings?

One explanation is that what lay people had thought to be inevitable—if they were to be "modern," efficient, and "of our times"—is now seen more realistically as the consequence of simple aesthetic choice. They believed the Movement's propaganda about the new architecture being a logical outcome of rational thought rather than just a fashion. They did not think there was an alternative.

The public has also learned that it is not helpless before the modern onslaught, and it has chosen to defend the parts of its architectural heritage that it values.

Finally, there is the mysterious element of taste, or fashion, which accepts something one year and rebels against it the next. We should not be surprised by these fickle shifts. Similar changes in aesthetic sensibilities have been responsible for the wildest swings of taste in the past. Consider the short time between Art Nouveau's enormous turn-of-the-century popularity on the Continent and the ascendancy of Josef Hoffmann, known in Viennese art circles as "Quadratl Hoffmann" (Hoffmann of the squares). In one lingering moment the electrifying whiplash of Art Nouveau had become nauseatingly rich, and the matter-of-fact meeting of perpendicular planes had replaced it as a source of elation and the essence of art.

Walnut armchair, Antonio Gaudi, ca. 1902 (The Metropolitan Museum of Art, Purchase, Joseph H. Hazen Foundation, Inc., Gift.)

Desk Set in ebony, leather, mother of pearl and silver, by Josef Hoffmann. Wiener Werkstätte, ca. 1910.

The Thread of Concern for Designing in Context

From the beginning, modernists tried to obliterate architectural history, both in theory and in practice. Their attack* on all non-modernist architecture was so violent and sweeping that, in retrospect, it seems impossible that any interest in a sympathetic relationship between new architecture and old could have survived. Yet a delicate thread of concern for these relationships did exist, and can be followed right through the modernist decades. While this book cannot present a full history of these ideas, it is appropriate to mention in passing something of what the counterculture to the Modern Movement has been thinking.

Arthur Trystan Edwards, the prominent English planner, wrote several books on architecture, the most pertinent to our discussion being *Good and Bad Manners in Architecture* (1923). It covers many aspects of this subject gracefully and perceptively and is worthwhile reading for anyone concerned with visual continuity in townscape.

Although we now know that the Modern Movement was alive and well in 1923, it had not yet had a strong impact in England. We listen with interest as Edwards rails on about architects' lack of sensitivity to the beauty of the street and, to our surprise, find that he is not talking about Le Corbusier, or Gropius, or Breuer, but about Norman Shaw, the Victorian architect who Edwards feels destroyed London's Regent Street with his late nineteenth century changes. Modernists did not write the book on how to disregard one's architectural neighbors, it would seem, although they did do the definitive edition.

Part of Edwards' case for a civilized, well-mannered urban architecture has been rendered moot by unforseeable advances in technology and the urban dweller's unsuspected ability to withstand crowding and chaos. He advances the touchingly prophetic argument that, if skyscrapers were ever allowed in London, they would reduce St. Paul's to insignificance. But, he says, the fireproofing problems and the insoluble difficulties of traffic congestion alone would surely rule them out.

Edwards' other observations remain as true now as then. The real problem, he says, is the expression of the architect's emotions (or as I will put it later, the display of the designer's ego) that so often disfigures a streetscape. He attributes the lack of continuity in modern towns to the architect's destructive individualism (ego) and to the fear of monotony that breeds a desire for novelty. Interestingly enough, he places the blame squarely on the professional. It is not commercial greed that destroys the city-scape, but the architect's refusal to use the power of his professional status to lead clients to the aesthetically sound solutions.

The illustrations he offers are interesting but, as the excesses of modernism have taken us so far beyond anything Edwards might have imagined, even in his most depressed state, they do not seem so shocking to us as they must have to him. We have grown accustomed to an almost total lack of continuity in urban architecture, and therefore we tend to view the most rudimentary attempts at reconciliation gratefully.

Good and Bad Manners in Architecture is a lovingly written, though tragically unheeded, plea for an urbane, respectful architecture; for architects to recognize that an individual building is always seen first as a part of the urban whole.

In *The Golden City* (1959), Henry Hope Reed also discusses townscape and the impact of modern architecture. He uses a graphic device similar to the one I employ in this volume: contrasting modern buildings with ones of an older style. But his juxtapositions exist only on paper; the buildings do not actually stand side by side as they appear in the book. In addition, the aim of his comparisons is notably different from that of this book. Reed wants to replace the modern style with a revival of

---

* "Architecture has for its first duty, in this period of renewal, that of bringing about a revision of values. . . . The styles of Louis XIV, XV, XVI or Gothic, are to architecture what a feather is on a woman's head. . . . The 'styles' are a lie." Le Corbusier, *Toward a New Architecture*. 1923.

American Classicism. The intention of *Architecture in Context* is to encourage designers in any style—revolutionary or conservative—to be aware that their work will be judged as a part of a larger physical context.

Continuity and Change: Preservation in City Planning (1971), by Alexander Papageorgiou, focuses on cities with extant historic cores. It contains valuable information about the changes taking place in these historic centers, although some of its conclusions—such as the prediction that urban megastructures represent the future of the city—are surely obsolete by now.

Others have written more recently about respecting the physical context. Colin Rowe, Tom Schumacher, and Alan Colquhoun, to mention a few, have explored the relatively large-scale issues of urban design: how the character of a city is reinforced or disrupted depending upon the types of buildings added and their relationship to the context. Much of this work has focused on figure-ground studies of city plans which alternately emphasize the buildings and the spaces between them. This is a helpful tool because we see the city in an unfamiliar way which forces a reappraisal of our opinions. But, while figure-ground studies can give an important overview, they alone cannot tell us about visual continuity. Configurations that seem integrated on a large-scale plan can easily fail to convince at the 1:1 scale of reality. The broader character of a city's plan may be less apparent, and less pertinent, when seen from the pedestrian's eye than from the bird's eye.

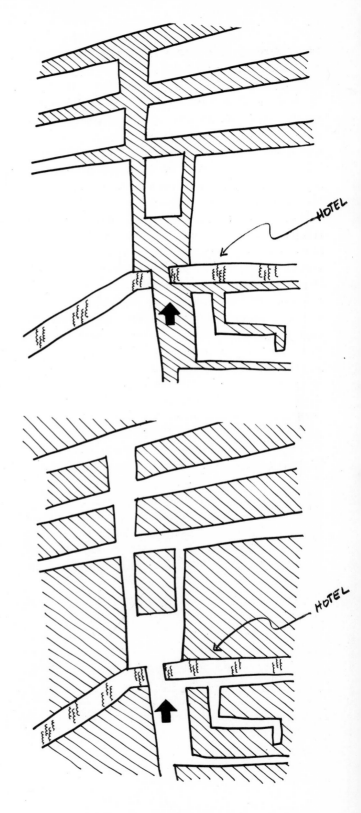

Figure/ground plans of Campo Moise, Venice, showing the site of the Bauer Grunewald Hotel. Arrows indicate view shown in the photograph of the Hotel.

14

Post-Modernism and Fitting New Architecture with Old

In the past ten or fifteen years the rules of the Modern Movement have come under direct attack. While the architects who now question that long-accepted catechism do not yet form a coherent group—in either style or ideology—they tend to be lumped together for what seem to be reasons of journalistic convenience into one category called "post-modern."

Robert Stern, an architect and writer, has said that post-modernists share a common interest in: 1) Contextualism: the possibility for the future expansion of a given building and the desire to relate it to the immediate surroundings. 2) Allusionism: references to the history of architecture which somehow go beyond "eclecticism" to a somewhat vague category called "the relationship between form and shape and the meanings that particular shapes have assumed over the course of time." 3) Ornamentalism: the simple pleasure in decorating architecture.

In spite of the first item on this list, the works of many post-modern architects seem as inattentive to their context as any of the preceding generation's. Therefore *Architecture in Context* does not speak about post-modernism as a movement, but only about specific buildings which offer something of interest to our topic.

New trends such as post-modernism grow out of normal changes in architectural *fashions*. The fact that equal weight is now given to a variety of aesthetic approaches, including the now-traditional modernism, is doubtless a reflection of the general uncertainty about which, if any, is the proper one.

Campo Moise, Venice, showing the Bauer Grunewald Hotel.
The figure/ground drawings reveal nothing of this
building's *visual* impact on its context.

Vertical skyscraper: Woolworth Building, Cass Gilbert (1913). New York City.

Horizontal Skyscraper, Emery Roth & Sons, New York City.

Vertical Skyscraper, General Motors Building, Edward Durell Stone; Emery Roth and Sons, Associated Architects (1968). New York City.

The rhetoric of these new groups often includes sincere words of concern for the relationship of their new architecture to its context. As with all theorizing, *Architecture in Context* included, these expressions of concern should not be taken at face value. A closer look at the buildings themselves may reveal ideologies which aim less at furthering contextual harmony than at promulgating a particular set of aesthetic preferences; discussion of the context comes only in terms of how it will be enhanced by the addition of buildings which follow *those* particular precepts.

Architecture in Context takes the point of view that the exclusive aesthetics postulated by these groups should be subordinated to the larger purpose of creating a civilized townscape in which new architecture is sympathetically integrated with old, regardless of the particular aesthetic bent of the new. I would urge that the architectural themes which are being explored by these groups be pursued within a broader philosophical framework, the aim of which is to create a visually integrated—not necessarily stylistically homogeneous—townscape. This holds true whether the context to be respected is modern or non-modern.

16

My assumption, based on observations of the pre-modernist townscape, is that new architectural fashions *can* harmonize with existing contexts without sacrificing their unique character. Any fashion, that is, except main-stream modernism, which has scorned ornament and other time-honored cultural symbols and rejected all eclecticism as proof of creative sterility.

Horizontal skyscraper. Citicorp Building, Hugh Stubbins (1978). New York City.

The whimsicality of architectural fashion is particularly evident in skyscraper design. The office skyscraper, for example, has continued pretty much the same functions ever since it was invented, in the late 19th century. It has also been designed with pretty much the same economic and use-related constraints—ratio of corridor to useable office space, number of elevators required to move the building's population, etc., and building techniques have changed only in detail: skyscrapers have always been supported by a structural frame—either steel or reinforced concrete—around which is fixed a thick or thin skin of masonry, metal, or glass. Yet skyscraper facade design changes with surprising regularity, architecturally speaking, shifting from horizontal to vertical dress about every decade or decade and a half, with occasional periods of relative balance which produce facades like those on the Seagram Building and Lever House.

The Purpose

It is evident that there will always be difficulties in agreeing on what fits into a given context. The problem is further complicated by the fact that a building which contrasts with the surroundings can sometimes be a desirable thing. *Architecture in Context* sets about relating our changing perceptions of the relationship between new and old to the way designers worked and onlookers perceived buildings before the advent of modernism. An understanding of how these visual relationships were established in the past will help inform our present and future choices.

My intention is not to revive historical styles but to revive a way of looking at the whole of the architectural context which will encourage architects, planners and entrepreneurs to consider thoughtfully the visual effects of additions to their surroundings.

The method of *Architecture in Context* is to consider the specific, small scale problems of relating new to old before those of a broader and therefore almost inevitably more abstract nature. I feel that lessons learned from small scale problems will foster improvements on the larger scene.

Above all, *Architecture in Context* is not a preservationist plea for the status quo. It does not urge the mummification of old towns, although that may sometimes be desirable. It is understandable that people who live in a neighborhood, and who see it as "home," rather than as an architectural setting, will resist change. But there is a significant difference between this habitual conservatism and the informed caution born of having repeatedly witnessed the destruction of once-cohesive visual neighborhoods by the insolent stylistic intrusions of modern architecture. The public's more militant conservatism may come from a *fear* of modern architecture rather than from an unwillingness to accept sensitive change. ("Sensitive" to what they see as the spirit of their neighborhood.) I have seldom seen a group of professionals more open to modernism (with less reason) than the hopeful preservationists attending the National Trust for Historic Preservation's 1977 Conference on fitting new architecture with old.

I believe that cultivating a greater degree of contextural awareness is an all-too-neglected task of today's architects, planners and builders. I did not arrive at this conviction through theorizing about the meaning of Architecture or the architect's vague philosophical and political responsibilities, but by looking around and realizing that visual continuity is a major component of the places I feel are beautiful. It will become clear from the following examples that architecturally felicitous relationships do not depend on copied architectural styles, or even on slavishly following some well-meant lists of design criteria, all too often today the first line of defense for those interested in maintaining a semblance of visual continuity in their communities.

To reachieve visual coherence in our architectural surroundings requires changing the way architects have been taught to see. It will also necessitate, as we shall see later, a delicate redefinition of "architectural creativity."

2

Historical Examples of Successful Fit-Ins

I have often had architects ask me questions like "If all you want is a building that mimics its neighbors, why use an architect?" (For *architect*, of course, read *creative artist*.) Contrary to the assumption implicit in this question, designing a building that is sympathetic to its context, in any era, has demanded creativity, skill and the judicious use of the craft of design. It has never depended on rote copying.

The millions of travelers who tour old European towns each year are not attracted solely by the romance of history. They are also drawn by the physical beauty of these places which springs in large part from their visual harmony. Although their architectural styles are rarely totally homogeneous, these old townscapes often give the impression of careful composition because of the pains taken over centuries to relate each new style to those that preceded it. An aesthetic regulator seems to have been at work guiding generations of anonymous designers and craftsmen in respecting the existing townscape without compromising the originality or quality of their own work. Broad sequences of styles are fused into a single, coherent architectural presence, yet this has been accomplished without sacrificing a building's own special character. Gothic, Renaissance and Baroque facades stand together happily in the medieval towns of southern Germany. Nineteenth century eclectic, eighteenth century baroque and twentieth century art deco co-exist without conflict in most larger European cities.

Persisting social customs, limitations on the availability of materials and standardized construction methods all helped to make some degree of visual integration inevitable in the pre-industrial world. The designer's own preferences, however, often seem to have been the deciding factor. While we seldom think of them in this way, each of the styles we now know as historical was, in its own time, modern. Contrary to today's common practice, these innovative modern styles were often carefully related to older architectural settings. Skilled designers *chose* to make sympathetic visual connections between their new buildings and older ones so that conflicts between potentially antagonistic styles seldom materialized. The fruits of this enlightened approach are visually rich, integrated streetscapes owing their unity not to the cliché of copying but to the sophisticated and uninhibited attention of generations who enlivened the street with varied yet compatible additions.

This intention is sometimes noted by contemporaries. Georgio Vasari mentions it, as we will note presently, when writing about Michelangelo's New Sacristy for San Lorenzo, the Medici church in

19

Florence. We do not know if other decisions were so consciously made. However, the very existence of such a high degree of refinement in towns with diverse architectural styles makes one feel that the question is almost irrelevant. Making visual connections between buildings of different periods seems to have been done simply because it was the obvious way to please the eye.

Today's designer, looking for ways to relate his architecture to its context, faces dilemmas not unlike those solved by his predecessors. The visual problems remain the same, regardless of the changes in materials and techniques. Even so, a surprising number of modern buildings still use materials like brick and wood that have been used in the same ways for centuries. The following historical examples are offered in a spirit of exploration to try to reacquaint us with this way of seeing architecture in relation to its surroundings. They should be used as reference points, a small catalogue of variations on visual themes that have had some success and therefore may be helpful now, as we address analogous problems in our changed circumstances.

Old Buildings with Landmarks

Old and New Sacristies, San Lorenzo, Florence (Filippo Brunelleschi, 1421–28; Michelangelo, 1521–34.)

"He wanted to execute the work in imitation of the old sacristy made by Filippo Brunelleschi but with different decorative features; and so he did the ornamentation in a composite order, in a style more varied and more original than any other master, ancient or modern, has ever been able to achieve. . .he broke the bonds and chains that had previously confined them to the creation of traditional forms." (*Lives of the Artists*, (1568), Vasari. Penguin, 1965, p. 366. George Bull, trans.)

Georgio Vasari was referring to the New Sacristy in the Florentine Church of San Lorenzo, designed by Michelangelo a century after Brunelleschi's Sacristy had been completed. Michelangelo solved the problem of linking new with old with a singularly rich mixture. While unquestioned respect for the old is immediately apparent, so too is a fierce originality in the new.

The broad relationship to Brunelleschi's work is clear; Michelangelo used the same contrast between light stucco walls and darker pilasters, entablatures and archivolts. This connection is so powerful that it allows us to accept the remarkably different architectural forms which he then introduces, since the initial impression of direct correspondence between old and new is deceptive. In fact only the lower pilasters are repeated in a near-original form.

Old Sacristy, San Lorenzo, Florence; Filippo Brunelleschi (1421–28).

The rope molding of the dome over Brunelleschi's altar, and the enriched torus moldings of the main arch and the entablature have been drastically simplified in the New Sacristy. The shell ornament in the altar pendentives has been reduced to plain circular moldings and the low relief sculpture is omitted entirely, focusing attention on the tomb figures. The New Sacristy is also a full story higher than the Old, bringing additional light into the chapel for the sculpture. The traditional architectural forms of Brunelleschi's niches and doorways are replaced by unique variations on traditional elements, and totally new inventions which astonished Michelangelo's contemporaries.

This is a brilliant "imitation" of the *feeling* of the Old Sacristy. Yet it is carried through with such inventive virtuosity that it becomes the exceptional architectural experience, a work simultaneously rich in tradition and newness.

New Sacristy (Medici Chapel) San Lorenzo, Florence; Michelangelo (1521–34).

Detail of New Sacristy showing simplified moldings.

Library of St. Marks and the Procuratie Nuovo, Venice (Jacopo Sansovino, 1536–53; Vicenzo Scamozzi, begun 1584.)

Next we note an instance where the client has decreed a more direct relationship between a new and (slightly) older building overruling the wishes of the architect. The Library of St. Marks, by Jacopo Sansovino, was completed in 1553. In 1585, Vicenzo Scamozzi won a competition for the Procuratie Nuovo, a long building to house the rulers of the city which was to form the south side of the Piazza.

Scamozzi's scheme called for separating his building from the Library so that he could use a new and different architectural order. The city fathers turned him down, preferring to continue the arcade of the Library as it was. Scamozzi yielded, but successfully integrated a three-story Procuratie Nuovo with the older Library which, because of structural reasons, had been limited to two stories.

Procuratie Nuovo, St. Mark's Square, Venice; Vicenzo Scamozzi (begun 1584).

Library of St. Mark's, Venice; Jacopo Sansovino (1536–53).

Westminster Hall and the Houses of Parliament, London (ca. 1097; Sir Charles Barry and A. W. N. Pugin, begun 1835.)

The original Westminster Hall was completed in the Eleventh Century; the present structure dates from a rebuilding in 1401. In 1834, the nearby buildings that had been occupied by Parliament for centuries burned down and a competition was held for the design of the now-familiar Houses of Parliament. The committee in charge of the competition specified that the design should be executed in the Gothic style.

While Gothic Revival architecture looms large in our view of the 19th century, it is interesting that, at the time of this competition, it was a relatively small movement. As Sir Kenneth Clark points out, while many Englishmen then thought of it as a national style, it had never before been used for a large secular building. (*The Gothic Revival*, Pelican Books, 1964. p. 99) Even at the Crystal Palace Exhibition of 1851, nearly twenty years later, only a relatively small space was allotted to the Medieval Hall.

According to Clark the committee for rebuilding the Palace at Westminster had "special reasons" for specifying that the new buildings should be in the Gothic style. Those reasons were rooted in considerations of context. Westminster Hall and a portion of the 14th century St. Stephens Chapel which survived the fire were both Gothic, and the great national symbol, Westminster Abbey (begun in 1052, but largely rebuilt in the 13th century) was literally next door. Insuring that the new Houses of Parliament would be compatible with these monuments was obviously only a matter of visual common sense.

Westminster Hall, London. Original building dates from 1097, renovated and roof rebuilt, 1397–99. Houses of Parliament, Sir Charles Barry and A. W. N. Pugin (begun 1835).

Town Hall and the Old Recorder's House,
Bruges, Belgium (1376–1420; 1535–37.)

The Town Hall of Bruges and the adjoining Recorder's House offer a striking example of how architectural styles with fundamentally contradictory characteristics can still be sympathetic. In this case, a small Renaissance building is reconciled with a Gothic neighbor over two times its height and a century its senior. The vertical emphasis of each building is the key to their sympathetic relationship. One expects verticality in a Gothic building, but it is more surprising in the Recorder's House because classically inspired buildings are usually serene and horizontal. Here, the verticality literally overlays an otherwise typical northern Renaissance facade.

Both buildings have a high proportion of window to wall, restricting their decoration to the relatively narrow areas between the openings. The Town Hall has pairs of small sculpture platforms with conical spires stacked one over the other. The windows are narrow and the second floor spandrel is recessed; this, and the continuous frame around both first and second story windows, makes them

(Right) Town Hall, Bruges, Belgium (1376–1420, restored 1853, 1959–62); (left) Old Recorder's House (1535–37).

look like one vertical unit. The turrets, elongated dormers and cresting reinforce this verticality and feather the building's silhouette into the sky.

The Recorder's House is composed of characteristically neo-classical forms. It is horizontally layered, with a different architectural order marking each floor, emphasized by appropriate horizontal entablatures. The window frames are contained within the height of each floor, unlike those of the Town Hall. The columns, however, with their plinths and entablatures, jut out from the facade making a continuous vertical line from ground to cornice that overrides the classically derived horizontal organization. In visual terms then, the engaged columns create the same vertical feeling as the continuous window frames of the Town Hall. The facade is topped by three exuberant scroll pediments which again emphasize the vertical and, with crockets and crowning statues, dissolve the building's bulk against the sky.

This sophisticated compositional compromise allows an appropriately detailed Flemish Renaissance building to look more vertical than horizontal, resolving the expected antagonism between two disparate styles.

Detail of Old Recorder's House and Town Hall, Bruges.

Gothic Versus Baroque

Few Gothic churches escaped the Counter-Reformation. Baroque altars, pulpits and other frothy extravagances were splashed into naves and apses all across the Continent. These invaders violently contradict the original character of the earlier churches, yet are usually absorbed with little difficulty.

The vast scale of Amiens Cathedral, for instance, controls the Baroque intrusion by overwhelming it.

In smaller churches, like St. Michaels, in Vienna, the cellular nature of Gothic vaulting isolates and contains the novelty.

Others are less fortunate, like the master mason of St. Stephen's, also in Vienna, who gazes wistfully at this misplaced addition to his composition.

Interior, St. Stephen's Cathedral (14th century, completely restored after World War II). Gothic interior, Baroque altar.

Interior, St. Michaels, Vienna (ca. 14th century). Gothic Chancel with Rococo "Fall of the Angels" by Jean Baptiste d'Avrange (1781).

Interior, Amiens Cathedral (nave completed 1236), with Baroque pulpit, ca. 17th century.

Rathaus, Rothenburg on the Tauber, Germany (Begun 1240; addition begun 1572.)

The Rathaus of Rothenburg was begun in 1240 and originally consisted of two long Gothic buildings side by side. In 1501, the easternmost building burned down and its ruins were finally cleared away and the present Renaissance building begun in 1572. In spite of the obvious differences between the primitive Gothic facade and its more sophisticated Renaissance neighbor, visual continuity was carefully maintained by the designer of the later structure. The two styles playfully use quite different architectural vocabularies to create the same visual feeling.

The domed tower of the older building, for example, gives the impression of symmetry. This is reinforced by the gable fenestration but, below the eave line, the window sizes change slightly: there are three large ones on the right and two smaller ones on the left. The imbalance increases as the eye moves farther down the facade, eventually coming to rest on the arched doorway that is unequivocally out of alignment.

The later building also teases the viewer with its near-symmetrical appearance. Its main entrance is directly under the gable but its onion-dome, at the corner, plays off against the gable windows which are tantalizingly close to being in balance. Symmetry, as with the earlier neighbor, eludes us entirely in the ground floor, with its quaint mother and child entrance.

The obvious discrepancies between these facades, including their different detail, color, and materials, are nevertheless resolved into an harmonious complementary relationship by their similar shape, Gothic and Renaissance pinnacles marching up their respective gables and by their whimsical "exchange" of motifs. A good example of the remarkable variety that can coexist with a sense of visual continuity.

Rathaus, Rothenburg on the Tauber. Gothic building (left)
(begun 1240), Renaissance building, Leonhard Weidmann,
(begun 1572).

Old Buildings Next to Older Buildings

Tom Tower, Christ Church College, Oxford, England (Sir Christopher Wren, 1681–82.)

When called upon to add a tower gate to Cardinal Woolsey's Great Quadrangle at Christ Church College, the 20 year old Christopher Wren, later to be called the greatest English Renaissance architect, matter-of-factly departed from the favored style of his day and produced a respectable Gothic tower to harmonize with the existing quadrangle, completed about 150 years earlier.

St. Barbara's, Vienna (Paul Sprenger, 1852.)

St. Barbara's, on the right, was completed by Paul Sprenger in 1852, two centuries after its neighbor on the left. These buildings are roughly the same height, have the same gold-colored stucco, but only share one string course out of a possible four. The genial compatibility of the relationship, however, gets extra enrichment from some discreet but significant differences.

The church facade is basically flat, compared to the three distinct planes of its larger neighbor. It substitutes arches for flat lintels and gently, rather than dogmatically, redirects the horizontality of its neighbor towards the vertical. It does this by the simple expedient of having fewer horizontal string courses and a small tower over its central entrance. A relatively simple, direct correspondence becomes more interesting because of subtle changes.

Tom Tower, Christ Church College, Oxford; Sir Christopher Wren (1681–82).

(Right) St. Barbara's, Vienna; Paul Sprenger (facade, 1852). Romanesque facade on the left, 1652–54.

Addition to a House on the Cathedral Square, Delft, Holland (ca. 19th Century.)

The second floor of this house was remodelled in the 19th century and became a 'window wall,' in contrast to the other buildings around the Square. In spite of the builder's flagrant disregard for present-day design criteria—maintaining window proportions and solid to void relationships, and using similar materials—the renovation has an eerie quality of belonging.

An initial, if faint, sympathy is established by the cast iron colonnettes that divide the facade into three parts, corresponding to the typical divisions of the other facades on the Square. But the main connection between the addition and its neighbor is an ingenious illusion: the glass panes and mullions of the addition repeat the same general pattern as the adjoining building's rustication, but in mirror image. In the glass wall the lines are raised and the planes recessed. The opposite is true of its solid counterpart.

Its two bands of gingerbread ornament are a surprise, and might be disturbing if they were not literally kept in line by being attached to a cornice above and a string course at mid-facade. Both cornice and string course continue elements of the next house.

This renovation would probably never have been passed by a contemporary design review board. It has an adventurous quality which few modern examples can match in the sureness with which it strikes out on its own while respecting the basic character of its context.

Addition to house on Cathedral Square, Delft, Holland, ca. 19th century.

Two Houses, Delft, Holland
A whimsical example of fitting in by embracing.

Cotton Exchange, Savannah, Georgia
(William Gibbons Preston, 1887.)

Both of these buildings are brick, but the Port Authority, on the left, has been painted white. The color difference is dramatic and, from what we are told about the importance of similar coloring for fitting in, should overshadow any relationship that might have been established by the shared material. Even so, the eye immediately connects them because it goes directly to the arch of the Exchange entrance and to those of the main bay and lower floors of the Port Authority building next door. Furthermore, the dominant-subordinate relationship helps to establish a connection. These two elements are enough to override what would ordinarily be a fatal difference in color.

Two houses, Delft, Holland (dates unknown).

Cotton Exchange, Savannah, Georgia; William Gibbons Preston (1887).

House and Addition, Nantucket Island, Massachusetts

The wing which was added to this house (on the right) introduces a new element into the problem of fitting new architecture with old: the selective eye which is guided by social convention and sees only what it is supposed to see. Notice the difference between the formal facade of this house (on the left) and the rest of the agglomeration. The formal facade, the part of the house which is "presented" to the rest of this very formal street, is symmetrical in every detail: double entrance stair, front door, windows, even the central panel on the widow's walk. But the rest of the house, all of which is quite as visible from the street as this facade, is treated in a totally different manner. Granted, the white trim and scale are consistent, but the windows are haphazardly placed and the material and color changes completely. The rules for fitting new with old which are generally accepted by designers and review boards today state that materials should be similar, as should the disposition of the doors and windows (if the openings are symmetrical on the old, they should be symmetrical on the new as well). Yet here even the side of this "presentation" facade is different, not to speak of the rest of the addition. Why, then, do we not object to these differences?

As I said, the scale and detail play their part. But they are not all. We have a distinctly non-architectural, non-visual element to contend with here: social convention. Everyone knows that the whole building, with all its ramblings, is visible from the street; but the unspoken consensus permits the less socially relevant parts of the house to be considered on a different aesthetic scale from the "presented" facade—in much the same manner as the owner of the house might dress one way when in the backyard and another when promenading on this main street.

House and addition, Nantucket, Massachusetts (dates unknown).

There are literally hundreds of thousands of examples of this kind in residential housing in this country and abroad. In towns which manufacture brick, the "presented" facades of the more important houses are usually of wood—the scarcer material—while the sides and backs are of brick. Where wood is plentiful the more socially prominent part of the house is usually of brick.

The important point for designers is that this is yet another instance where the accepted rules governing the relationship between new and old do not apply. Here, however, the break is not visual but sociological. The eye *sees* the difference but social convention tells us not to pay any attention. Hence the question of relating even the various parts of the same building, in material and composition, cannot always be considered in purely visual terms.

Old Buildings with Older Neighborhood or Regional Styles

Streetscape, Haarlem, Holland

Streets such as this one are visually unified yet still offer a surprising variety. Gothic, Renaissance, Baroque, 19th and 20th century styles stand graciously side by side with considerable differences in cornice heights, roof silhouettes, window shapes and details. There are six different kinds of windows in this photograph, and such variety is the rule rather than the exception. Visual continuity obviously does not depend on stylistic conformity. Doctrinaire post-modernists of course have already said that we need not copy, but what they did not tell us was that fitting in does not necessarily depend on such things as facade proportion or maintaining the cornice height or silhouette,

Street, Haarlem, Holland (buildings from the 14th to the 20th century).

etc. This is clear when a sympathetically proportioned modern facade is inserted in such a traditional Dutch street. It maintains the proper height, silhouette and commercial ground floor treatment, but its interpretation of the traditional trim is totally out of character.

It is apparent that small scale detail resolves many of the larger scale differences on this Haarlem street. The most important element is the ubiquitous white trim outlining the windows and highlighting cornices, dormers, brackets and other details; its overall richness allows the street to absorb substantial variations that would otherwise be disruptive, such as the changes in style, color, materials and building height.

Early Dutch modernists recognized the healing power of this trim and many potentially awkward buildings of that period owe their limited success at fitting in to continuing this tradition.

MODERN TRIM — OUT OF STYLE

New and old, Zwolle, Holland.

Vroom & Dreesman Department Store, Haarlem, Holland; Jan Juijt, Architect (1937).

Streetscape, Vienna

In few cities is the importance of consistent surface texture more apparent than in Vienna, where the facades in the old city have a richness comparable only to the local pastries. Cornices, brackets, pediments, ballustrades, rustication and other details create a voluptuous surface texture bridging all styles with the predictable exception of the modern intrusions. Non-modern buildings, including 20th century Art Deco, maintain the general harmony by using their dissimilar parts in similar ways. This automobile garage shows how easily continuity can be disturbed when that texture is interrupted.

Parking garage, Vienna (ca. 1950s).

When the alternative is inserted, we no longer find ourselves looking at an [architectural] object in an irrelevant setting, but are once again able to appreciate the entire context, the architectural ensemble. (Photomontage: Angus Macdonald.)

Vienna.

34

Three Houses, Bruges, Belgium

These three facades are closely related in visual terms although their styles are different: from left to right, Gothic, Rococo and Baroque. The most obvious discrepancy is the ornament, shown clearly in the gable ends. The facades also have different finishes; the Gothic facade is brick while the others have their brick covered with stucco.

These considerable stylistic differences are counterbalanced by similarities in height and proportion of window to wall. We might expect such a mixture to produce a visual jumble, as so often happens when modern architecture is shuffled in with other styles. Instead, the three form a congenial composition because they share a number of visual themes. Although no single building has all the motifs, the interweaving binds them together.

The Rococo and Baroque facades, for instance, have a similar color and finish; the Gothic is different. Gothic and Rococo have applied ornament over their windows (in different styles) while the other is virtually without ornament. Gothic and Baroque have accented gables (in different styles), while the third is topped with a flat Italianate cornice. The Rococo and Baroque facades have similar string courses that are omitted on the Gothic. Both Gothic and Rococo have pronounced curves at the windows while the Baroque lintels only flex tentatively at the second story.

The ornament is different on each facade, but its *placement*—around the windows, at the gables and string courses—and its *visual character*—the use of curves in theme and variation—moderate the stylistic differences. Careful modulation of the ornament tends to unify the facades with a similar visual texture.

Three houses, Bruges, Belgium (dates unknown).

Houses, Strasbourg, France

The first impression of visual cohesiveness among these houses belies their actual dissimilarities. The two on the left retain their medieval half-timbering. The next two have been remodelled into one facade with only a hint of the old decoration around the windows, a painted frame recalling the half-timbering. A narrower, Italianate house with shutters and a pedimented dormer follows and the group is finished off by the long, horizontal facade and string courses of a much more massive building that emphatically contrasts with the narrow, vertical fronts. Furthermore, these string courses run haphazardly into the windows of its narrower neighbor where its three main floors meet an adjoining four. Everything in this interesting block seems to violate the presently accepted practice of maintaining floor heights and keeping a similar directionality in neighboring facades, yet it clearly appears as a unit. There are three different kinds of windows in this block, and four basic facade-types, yet the group remains a sympathetic visual ensemble.

Two things account for most of the success: the rooftops and the street level rhythms. The disparate window types, colors, building heights and styles of decoration are sandwiched in between two layers that are slightly more consistent: the steeply sloped slate roofs with their open dormers for sausage-smoking, and a nearly continuous arcade motif at ground level.

The top and bottom of the sandwich are not all that make the mixture work. The facades differ stylistically, but they do share a refinement of detail and scale that give them a similar visual texture.

Houses on the Cathedral Square, Strasbourg, France (dates unknown).

Arcades, Padua, Italy

Although the arches, stories, and cornices are of different heights, widths and shapes, the familial resemblance is obvious, and hence the sense of continuity is strong.

Padua, Italy (dates unknown).

Conclusion

Designing with sympathy towards the context seems to have been a commonplace occurrence in the past. From the vigor and variety of the foregoing examples it is also abundantly clear that this attitude towards respecting the surroundings did not inhibit the designer's creativity or originality.

The general belief, as evidenced in today's architectural practice, seems to be that ornament is the least important element in relating new buildings to old. A related assumption is that establishing general similarities between new and old—such as similar heights, similar materials, similar massing—alone will guarantee a friendly relationship.

These historical examples, on the contrary, have shown that general similarities may really be less important than we have been led to believe. (See Faculty Club, U.C.S.B., page 87). With regard to height, for instance, the Recorder's House, in Bruges, is less than half as tall as the adjacent Town Hall (page 24), yet it establishes a thoroughly compatible relationship.

Ornament, and the visual texture and associations it creates, often seems to be a surer way to build a sympathetic visual relationship between buildings. This is true regardless of the style of the buildings, as we will see in later chapters.

3

New Buildings with Other New Buildings

While modernists have shown little interest in relating their work to older contexts, they have been less obstinate about it when the context is modern.

Housing, Weissenhof Housing Settlement, Stuttgart, Germany (1927); *right,* Mies van der Rohe, *left,* J. J. P. Oud.

Workers' Housing, Weissenhof, Stuttgart, Germany (Various architects, 1927.)

Weissenhof was a showplace of modern architecture in 1927; a number of the Movement's most important architects contributed buildings to this model settlement. The ideology which limited modernism's formal vocabulary made fitting with their own kind a relatively simple matter. This photograph shows the back of Mies van der Rohe's apartment block (right) and the entrances to row houses by J. J. P. Oud.

City Hall and The John F. Kennedy Federal Building, Boston (Kallmann, McKinnell and Knowles, 1968 and T. A. C., 1966)
The Albany Mall, Albany (Harrison & Abromowitz, 1976)
Upper Sixth Avenue, New York City (Various architects, ca. 1970s.)

In each of these examples, new relates to new with obvious ease. The linear motifs, some structural and some not, become ornamental patterns linking the buildings. They give little hint, however, of the comfortable variety that can exist in a friendly grouping of different types of buildings, and are almost totally devoid of detail which might give a clue to their overall scale.

(Right) Boston City Hall; Kallmann, McKinnell & Knowles
(1968); (left) J. F. K. Federal Building; The Architects Col-
laborative with Samuel Glaser Assocs. (1966).

Upper Sixth Avenue, New York City (ca. 1970s).

Albany Mall; Harrison & Abromowitz (1976).

State University of New York, Purchase (Edward Larabee Barnes, master planner, 1978.)

The SUNY Campus at Purchase, completed in 1978 under the general architectural direction of Edward Larabee Barnes, illustrates the negative side of visual consistency: boredom. One of the difficulties may be that, having ignored the importance of relating new buildings to their surroundings for so long, we tend to be unnecessarily timid in approaching the problem. Unsure of how to harness the potential for variety with compatibility which existed in the past, lockjaw of the mind sets in and we make uniformity the measure of harmony: use only one material and use it in the same way; keep cornice lines consistent when the program permits; orient all buildings identically towards the central space. Then, fearful that this already stultifying consistency might still be too confusing, the few remaining differences are masked by a monotonous covered walkway of sleep-inducing dimensions.

A richer ensemble would have been possible if we were more skilled in the art of relating different kinds of buildings. Just changing the brickwork pattern provides a refreshing variation. Venturi and Rauch's modest building becomes an oasis in this architectural wasteland by virtue of a simple glazed brick pattern on its plaza facade.

State University of New York, Purchase (SUNY); Master planner, Edward Larabee Barnes; buildings by various architects (1978).

Covered walkway, SUNY.

Louvain University, Louvain La Neuve, Belgium (1970s)

The buildings of the new campus of Louvain University are all in a contemporary style, but do not suffer from the bland uniformity of SUNY. There is a flexibility, variety and sense of continuity among these varied, modern buildings. The grand arches of the railroad station, for example, are referred to discreetly in the ground level detailing of the facing building. These are small things but the eye notices them and, as they accumulate in our visual memory, contributing to a feeling of harmony and a strong sense of place.

Louvain La Neuve University, Belgium (1970s).

Ornamental brickwork, Humanities Classroom Building; Venturi & Rauch (1972).

4

The Modernist Point of View:
Contrasting New with Old

Modernists who preached the demise of historical styles were myopically optimistic about what they saw as the new, gloriously inevitable future of architecture. Bolstered by what now seem naive sociological predictions—within a few decades everyone was supposed to live in giant apartment blocks and cook in communal kitchens—their religious faith in the Movement made them supremely secure in rejecting a benighted and ignorant past. These earnest revolutionaries simply could not imagine that traditional buildings would retain any meaning in their brave new architectural world.

Contrast: Addition to the Banacerraf House, Princeton, New Jersey; Michael Graves (1969).

Contrast: Wool Building, Carlton Gardens, St. James, London
(ca. 1965).

Contrast: Kingston, Jamaica.

Contrast: New York City.

Contrast: Bavarian Bauhaus.

Contrast. . .

The moral code of the Modern Movement as preached by Le Corbusier and Gropius* forbade using historical references in design. They were deemed "dishonest" because they did not conform to the architects' narrow definition of what constituted the "spirit of the times." Eschewing historical forms, modern architects then had no choice when it came to putting a new building next to an older one. They could not make a stylistic connection, so they had to "contrast" with the older structure. Architectural writing of the past half-century is littered with phrases like "the striking juxtaposition of. . ." and "the sharp contrast between. . . ." The expectation in bluntly confronting old with new is that we will be stunned into enthusiastic acceptance by the very shock of it. No doubt when this is skillfully and audaciously done it can be powerful. But obviously the potency of these contrasts decreases as their frequency increases; they make an impact only when they are the exception. Unfortunately they have become the rule. Our cities are peppered with them and the result is chaos rather than drama. (See also the discussion of Monuments, page 137.)

Contrast, as opposed to harmony, continues to have a strong appeal to architects. For one thing, it has been the only "professional" choice for so many years that it is the only solution most living architects know. But there is another aspect to the idea of contrasting which should not be underestimated. It concerns the convenience of such an approach to the designer. Without fear of being considered irresponsible—and in the vague hope of being thought more creative—architects can sidestep a difficult design problem and declare that they have established a relationship through contrast no matter what they design. Obtuse, ill-considered confrontations are routinely passed off with this reasoning, often to the bewilderment of the public. What is often no relationship at all has been touted as an aesthetically acceptable alternative.

Not to labor the obvious, we can begin to see that the mere creation of visual polarities does not absolutely guarantee visual interest. More often than not, in fact, the result simply looks like two unrelated buildings that happened to bump into one another. The viewer is hard put to differentiate between "contrasting with" and "ignoring."

. . .And the Link

In the pre-modernist past it was not uncommon to butt additions directly into existing buildings. Contemporary architects, however, have hesitated to make such direct contact with history. Modern Movement disciples ostensibly opposed any concession to the past, yet like architects of other eras, the modernists had highly developed visual sensitivity and thus little tolerance for certain kinds of visual chaos. Their compulsion for neatness and simplicity meant that they could not ignore the potential for confusion that existed when adding their sleek new designs to older buildings. They dealt with this problem by inserting a return—sometimes called a "link"—between the old and the new. When I was studying at Yale, it was common for critics to suggest we use the return whenever we did not know how to resolve the visual conflict between our designs and existing buildings.

There are several types of links. Some are true returns, set back from the facade plane. These can be as narrow as a few inches or as wide as ten or fifteen feet, depending on the size of the building. The link can also be flush with the old facade but of a different material from either old or new.

The link is both a literal drawing-back from the existing facade, and a symbolic withdrawal from the past. The modern vocabulary is erased at the point of contact leaving a neutered surface and the illusion that the two buildings have not really met.

---

* "A breach has been made with the past, which allows us to envision a new aspect of architecture corresponding to the technical civilization of the age we live in; *the morphology of dead styles has been destroyed*; and we are returning to honesty of thought and feeling." Walter Gropius, *The New Architecture and the Bauhaus*, MOMA, 1937 (Italics mine)

THE LINK BARELY TOUCHES

OLD

NEW

Interior view of "link" connecting the Helen D. Lockwood Library and its addition; Hellmuth, Obata & Kassabaum, Vassar College, Poughkeepsie, New York (1976). (Notice how the link tries to touch new and old as little as possible.)

The word "link" is, of course, a misnomer. It is a classic case of ignoring the visual reality to maintain the myth of contextual concern. The link does not *connect* at all, it merely pleads no contest and tries to pretend that the hostile elements never collided.

Well aware of the potential for conflict, designers sometimes opt to be as unobtrusive as possible by withdrawing as far as possible. While not a sophisticated solution, it is often the least offensive alternative if the rigidity of the designer's philosophy rules out a more direct and sympathetic relationship. It says "I am new, but I am trying, as best I can, to keep a respectful distance." The extent of withdrawal can be considerable. The 1960s A.I.A. Headquarters, in Washington, D.C., presses against the lot line to get as far away as it can from the Federal period Octagon House, as if somewhat embarrassed to be there at all.

The following examples show various approaches to contrasting and linking new and old.

"Link" between the Main Building, James Renwick (1865) and the Vassar College Center (1977). The Main Building, in the French II Empire Style, is on the National Register. Addition by Shelpey Bulfinch Richardson and Abbott.

Grace Building (left), New York City; S. O. M. (1972).

Less Successful Examples

Arts For Living Center, Henry Street Settlement, New York City (Prentice & Chan, 1974.)

The basic nature of the new Arts For Living Center challenges that of the old Henry Street Settlement. The latter is a simple shape made more complex and interesting through ornament. The new building is a complex shape made deadly dull by its lack of relieving detail, made confusing by its haphazard window holes and purposeful facing away from its parent, and made unbelievable by critics who claimed that it fit *well* with its neighbor.

Royal College of Physicians, London (Denys Lasdun, 1964.)

This is architecture as object, the typical modernist approach which ignores what is to the left and right. Cambridge Terrace (left, 1875) was no doubt also an unwelcome Victorian invader in its time, as the terrace housing around Regent's park was visually consistent, all having been designed or approved by John Nash in the 1820s. But the 1964 College of Physicians offers no way out of the design dilemma posed by this early infringement. It only exacerbates the situation.

Arts for Living Center, Henry Street Settlement, New York City; Prentice & Chan (1974).

Cambridge Terrace and Royal College of Physicians, London.

Detail of Royal College of Physicians (right); Denys Lasdun
(1964) and Cambridge Terrace (1875), London.

Beinecke Rare Book Library, Yale University, New Haven, Connecticut (S. O. M., 1963)

The Beinecke Library uses the separationist approach. This block-like jewel box, which might be an impressive building in its own right, forms the third wall of a U-shaped plaza opening onto Wall Street in the heart of the campus. The plaza is defined by three monumental buildings (including the Library), two of which, Freshman Commons and Woodbridge Hall, sport Beaux Arts' detailing and therefore have some sympathy towards one another.

The panoramic view shows the Library to be a bizarre intruder. It lays claim to as much territory as possible in order to separate itself from its architectural neighbors, claiming this ground by covering it with the same gray paving stone that creeps up its own supporting pylons. The plaza acts as an extension of the library, pushing a fortress-like wall up against Freshman Commons while two more embankments guard the streets to the side and rear, warding off an assortment of other styles. In actuality the library sits in the middle of one large, horizontal "return." But the attempt to separate it from its surroundings is defeated by the nearness of its neighbors. They are simply too close to be successfully ignored and Beinecke thus becomes an awkward ark run aground on a shoal of its own making.

Beinecke Rare Book Library and Woodbridge Hall.

Panoramic view of, (left to right) Beinecke Rare Book Library (S. O. M., 1963), Freshman Commons and Woodbridge Hall, Yale University.

Carpenter Center for the Visual Arts, Harvard University, Cambridge, Massachusetts (Le Corbusier, 1963.)

Carpenter Center does not fit in and doubtless was not intended to, but it is worth looking at because of the skillful means by which it separates itself from its context. By understanding the means of separation we learn something about possible ways to make connections.

Carpenter Center stands apart immediately because it is the only building on the block whose facade is not parallel to the street. Its main bulk is also pulled back from the streetline; only a soft, visually yielding shape pushes forward to compete with the neo-Georgian Fogg Art Museum on one side and the Federal style Faculty Club on the other. The eye slides around this form rather than being challenged as it would have been by a hard corner.

Approaching from the right we see this rounded

form and a relatively unobtrusive ramp. The latter curves up into the main building, whose considerable bulk is made less imposing by being broken into small pieces that step back from the street. The brise-soleil, although hardly appropriate to Cambridge winters, also eat into the building's visual solidity. Please note that this sort of fragmentation does not guarantee that a building will defer to its neighbors. Paul Rudolph's Art and Architecture Building, at Yale, is quite fragmented *and* quite aggressive. But Carpenter Center manages to be retiring without losing strength.

For all its modernity, Carpenter Center does not suffer from one chronic problem of contemporary buildings: a boring skyline. Its free-standing columns and beams and broken massing give its roofline variations similar to the more traditional buildings around it.

Carpenter Center for the Visual Arts; Le Corbusier, with Sert, Jackson & Gourley (1963), and The Fogg Museum (left).

Carpenter Center makes no effort to relate but at least respects the context by expressing its differentness in ways which cause the least direct confrontations. The architect's skill can be appreciated all the more by noting the primitive sore thumb relationship between the 1971 Gund Hall ziggurat, just down the street, and Memorial Hall, a Civil War monument of Beaux Arts persuasion.

Gund Hall (Graduate School of Design) (left); John Andrews/Anderson/Baldwin (1971) and Memorial Hall; Ware and Van Brunt (1870), Harvard University.

Doorways, Savannah, Georgia (19th and 20th centuries.)

Modern architecture strikes again. It is difficult to imagine a more inappropriate choice of materials (white stucco in a cast iron storefront) and composition (the only asymetrical element in a facade several blocks long). The modern windows on the right are less disturbing because they are more innocuous. (The new doorway leads to an architect/planner's office!)

Doorways, Waterfront Renewal, Savannah, Georgia (19th and 20th centuries).

Addition to the Bavarian State Library, Munich, Germany (Ruf, Döllgast, Kirsten, Werner, 1965.)

Note the careful alignment of string courses and floor heights, intellectualizations that do little to save this 1965 addition. A simple graphic device, such as reusing the arch motif of the old building, would doubtlessly have been more effective, regardless of whether the floor heights were maintained.

Department Store, Regensburg, Germany (ca. 1960s.)

This situation presented, in fairness, a difficult problem. The architect's choice lay between literally harmonizing with history, or trying to make a modern building serve as background. The architect chose the latter, but although the new building is neutral in terms of its detail, it is in no way retiring. It looks like a gigantic automobile compacter, about to crush the out-of-date Renaissance facade.

Addition to the Bavarian State Library, Munich, Germany; S. Ruf, H. Döllgast, H. Kirsten, G. Werner (1965).

Department Store, Regensburg, Germany (ca. 1960s).

An alternative might be to associate gently the new with the old. (Photomontage: Angus Macdonald.)

The main problem is its massing. If the new blocks had been lower than the central one, they might appear to be less threatening. Their lesser bulk would also be more in keeping with their less interesting surface texture. Even so, they might still seem to be holding the old facade hostage.

If the program did not permit less volume (even though there is an empty arcade under the left-hand block) one might have tried giving these new elements some modest traditional detailing reminiscent of the Renaissance building, as in the alternate design. Nothing so elaborate as to compete with it, but the new forms would seem less aggressive as they become more closely related.

Sears Crescent and Center Plaza, Boston (Original, 19th century, renovated by Stull, Assocs., 1969; Welton Becket, 1966–69.)

The relationship between Sears Crescent and Center Plaza illustrates a fundamental difference between modernist and non-modernist architecture which often inhibits a sympathetic relationship.

These buildings represent opposing conceptions. Center Plaza is gigantic and sweeping; it is perhaps twice the breadth of Sears Crescent and sadly lacks the latter's personality. It seems endless with so little visual interest that one's eye lights elsewhere with relief. Conceived as a continuum, it is one

slice of a giant wheel that has been overlayed with a uniform pattern to camouflage the joints. The attempt to relieve its dreary progress along the street by periodically raising the roofline only demonstrates the architect's awareness of his problem in venturing too timid a solution. The facade is an endless band holding little interest for the eye; we grasp it and then look past. By rights its very size should intimidate, but it does not. It bores.

Sears Crescent though undistinguished architecturally, is balanced, organically developed, and composed in the sense of having a left, middle, and right, a top, middle, and bottom. It is even dignified in an anthropomorphic way as it takes its stand facing the vast City Hall Plaza. From left to right, there is a low wing, a slightly higher center section with arched windows, and another low wing. Vertically there is a fancy lower floor, a rather plain mid-section and an attic story squeezed in between a cornice and string course. These simple devices create a clear focus and enliven a facade which, potentially, could have been as boring as that of Center Plaza.

Sears Crescent Building (left), rehabilitated by Stull, Associates (1969) and Center Plaza, Welton Becket & Associates (1966–69), Boston.

College Center, Vassar College, Poughkeepsie, New York (Shepley Bullfinch Richardson and Abbott, 1977.)

Aside from the gesture of using similar materials, the exterior of the new College Center has little to do, visually, with its older counterpart; the all too common link disavows any connection. Inside it is a different story. The new building is not a new appendage but an architectural slipcover, encasing an older wing.

The skylit interior is pleasant enough, but the blunt contrast between the thick members of new roof structure and the refined details of the old wing is disturbingly crude. It is most noticeable where the swollen beams, surprisingly large for their short span and light load, thud into the old brick wall. These clumsy, unarticulated blocks of metal come so close as to seem to endanger the delicate brick arches and spider webs of leaded glass. An unnecessarily heavy-handed institutional modern addition violates the modest but refined, humanly scaled architecture of the earlier building.

The problem here is not even one of conflicting historical styles. It is one of conflicting *visual character*—an unfeeling conjunction of two kinds of architecture with no family resemblance. One is light, the other ponderous; one witty, the other dull. A simple greenhouse structure would have had a more appropriate visual lightness.

Interior of College Center, showing the old wing of the Main Building, around which it is built.

Vassar College Center, Vassar College, Poughkeepsie, New York; Shepley Bulfinch Richardson and Abbott (1977) and the Main Building; James Renwick (1865).

Assembly Hall, Phillips Exeter Academy, Exeter, New Hampshire (Hardy Holzman Pfeiffer, 1968.)

The balcony addition to this auditorium is an exuberant example of the art of audacious architectural contrast. The problem was to insert a balcony into a strongly stated older space. As we can see by what remains of the old auditorium, its surfaces were organized traditionally with static panels defined by moldings dividing them into clearly bounded areas. Most of the wall and ceiling panels that described the old space are untouched. They bespeak the master craftsman's T-square and compass and are placed in our historical consciousness by their classically derived moldings, tondos and domes.

The new balcony is also firmly anchored, but in the most raw, contemporary iconography. It is freeway modern, the ribbon of Route 40 turned into a banked raceway, inviting the eye to whiz through the dignified old space with a playful thumb of the nose at the school fathers gazing from its walls. It is as clear a statement of the great American open road as any of Whitman's images.

The chrome-plated columns, defined only by changing reflections, reinforce the transitory feeling. The eye does not rest on them easily. And new curving benchbacks only heighten the sense of movement and undermine the old stability.

Assembly Hall, Phillips Exeter Academy, Exeter, New Hampshire; Hardy Holzman Pfeiffer Assocs. (1968).

This duel of contrasts encompasses details as well. The classical moldings are organized by the architect's hand and refined by the craftsman. The new ornament (see underside of the balcony) is also orchestrated by the designer, but the pleasure in the craftsman's touch is replaced by an unfortunate fascination with construction left-overs: the "honestly" expressed end of the channel that is cut off roughly after rounding the last turnpike bend, the unfiled welds, the bolted connections and corrugated steel decking.

These contrasts are indeed startling, but only half successful. To pull this off properly the new vocabulary should have met the old along clearly defined battle lines that remained consistent over a large area. Instead small engagements fragment the drama. Thus the chrome columns at the rear, that have sacrificed their capitals for improved visibility, are isolated from the main forces and appear awkward. The contrast is also weakened where some of the traditional ceiling panels have been scraped away to introduce new lighting, leaving occasional naked areas on an otherwise articulated ceiling.

The grand sweep of the balcony itself is the strongest and hence perhaps the least offensive element. This is in part because the eye slides over it quickly and easily and in part because it is one simple unit, clearly separated over a large expanse from the visual complexities of the earlier design.

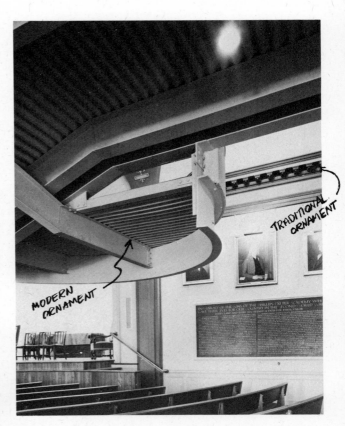

Detail of Assembly Hall showing modern and traditional ornament.

Another view of Assembly Hall.

More Successful Examples

Castelvecchio Museum, Verona, Italy (Carlo Scarpa, 1958–61.)

Carlo Scarpa's renovation of this museum is a model of artful contrast. The interior is modern, the exterior seemingly untouched. But look more closely at the arched opening in the center of the overall view. A strange wall cuts across it, changing height almost in the center of the opening. The same thing happens behind the arcade on the far right. The mullions above both these walls seem to be arranged casually. But are they new or old?

At the far left the truth literally comes out as the old building is peeled away. Ancient tiles stop and a contemporary roof continues. The masonry wall ends irregularly, its stucco cut away, offering a vignette of old stone and brick; from there on the roof is supported by a bare steel column. An equestrian statue stands under the modern roof, supported by the present—a reinforced concrete cantilever—but facing the past. It is strong and poignant, a poetic contrast of then and now.

Detail, Castelvecchio Museum, Verona.

Castelvecchio Museum, Verona, Italy; Carlo Scarpa (1958–61).

Exeter Theater, Boston (Childs, Bertman, Tseckares, 1977.)

Some combinations of materials, like this steel and glass "greenhouse," seem to be sympathetic to many different contexts. Here the smoothness and lightness contrast nicely with the roughness and weight of the stone.

New York State Bar Association, Albany (James Stewart Polshek and Assocs., 1971.)

One of the better ways to solve the problem of fitting new with old is to avoid it. The Civil War period townhouses to the left face onto a square near the State House. Their facades have been left intact while their interiors and rear prospects were rebuilt in 1971 in a completely modern idiom. The Janus solution succeeds here by virtue of its discretion.

Exeter Theater, Boston; Childs, Bertman, Tseckares (1977).

New York State Bar Association, Albany; James Stewart Polshek and Assocs., (1971).

5

New Buildings with Nearby Buildings

Many recently awakened design review boards and planning commissions have compiled lists of design criteria for new architecture which must harmonize with old. The best of these lists are perceptive and informative, yet a mere list can also be misleading. First, it tends to create the expectation that following such a list guarantees a good fit. This, as we have been discovering, is not necessarily true. Second, nearly all of these lists are tainted by modernist prejudices against historical styles and ornament, often the most helpful tools for building a good connection.

However, Paul Muldawer, in cooperation with the planning firm of Eric Hill Associates, has developed one of the most complete and useful lists of criteria as part of an H.U.D. funded study of Savannah, Georgia. This list is interesting because it includes, on an equal footing with other frequently mentioned requirements such as maintaining "visually compatible" cornice lines and materials, the need to respect the "relationship of architectural *details*" (my emphasis) such as cornices, lintels, arches and so on. (Presumably this could refer to details of any style, modern or traditional.) The importance of small scale details, which were enjoyed in the past for their purely ornamental qualities, is routinely underplayed when it is not omitted entirely from contemporary lists of design criteria. Their rightful inclusion here may be due to the nature of the subject matter; Savannah is one of the country's architectural treasures. However, the rigor it demands in terms of attention to relating architectural details should not waver in places of less obvious value.

It is worth mention that the same Historic Preservation Bulletin that carries Muldawer's list includes two other articles claiming that detail is the *least important* factor in relating one building to another whether or not one is designing in an historical area. So much for clear thinking!

Most lists of design criteria that are intended to guide renovations in historic districts, as opposed to new construction, naturally do mention appropriate details or ornament. But resolve seems to fail when it comes to inserting new designs; these strict requirements are inexplicably undercut although there is no logical reason why ornament should be helpful in renovations and not in new buildings. A report on design criteria for restoration and new design in Galena, Illinois, for example, recommends using traditional stone or brick cornices in new construction, then obscures this common sense by cautioning against "eclecticism." What is a traditional brick cornice that is not eclectic?

This peculiar confusion of logic is commonplace today. It is a perplexingly perverse attitude that acknowledges the need to relate through details

a

b

c

and then plays down the importance of ornament, although this is the simplest and most effective way to establish such a relationship. That ornament need not be purely eclectic almost goes without saying; it can be completely original, modern ornament, so long as it captures the *visual spirit* of the original.

Such self-defeating inhibitions emphasize the predicament of many conscientious designers who cannot wholly shake off the anti-ornamental mantle of "less is more." Because of these persistent inhibitions, the standards by which new/old relationships are judged have remained undeveloped. It is not surprising, therefore, that even the most earnest recent attempts to fit new with old have been only partially successful.

The general assumption seems to be that if one can establish a visual quorum—by satisfying enough of the criteria on the list—a good relationship will be legislated. As we have seen before, the problem is not so easily resolved. A building that differs in ways so often thought to be critical, including its height, proportions and materials, can still be congenial if its visual texture, in large part created by its small scale detail or ornament, is consistent with that of its neighbors. Ironically, the closer a building comes to copying a neighbor in material, scale, proportion, height and so on, the more naked and out of place it seems when it omits the ornamental particulars.

The "before" and "after" sketches (*a* and *b*) appear in Lowell: *The Building Book*, a conscientious and thorough guide to fitting new buildings into the streetscapes of Lowell, Massachusetts. The problem is that the "after" version does not go far enough; it captures the rhythm and proportion of the older buildings but still looks out of place because it is naked. Adding ornament to it (*c*) brings it completely into the fold and makes it a much more compatible neighbor. The trouble is that few professionals are able—yet—to bring themselves to this [visually] obvious step. It is a step, by the way, which is obvious to nearly all laypeople. (Photomontage: Brent C. Brolin.)

Less Successful Examples

Jehovah's Witnesses Building, Brooklyn Heights, New York (Ulrich Franzen Assocs., 1970.)

When I first saw the Jehovah's Witnesses Building in the Bulletin of the National Trust I assumed it had been offered as an example of what not to do. Upon reading the text, I was surprised to find it was considered an excellent example of fitting new with old.

The New York City Landmarks Commission exercised considerable influence in choosing this design. The sponsor originally proposed a "Georgian" building, but it was thought by the Commission to be too "pretentious." (For some inexplicable reason, official bodies which rule on design tend to see pretentiousness as a vice from which only old buildings suffer, when a glance around shows that it is one of the most pronounced characteristics of modern architecture.) The architect then presented a series of alternate designs, all of which were eclectic and all of which were rejected.

The Commission ultimately asked Ulrich Franzen to act as design consultant and his was the final design; it was lauded in the Preservation Bulletin as not compromising itself in style (i.e., it was a strong personal statement which made no historical references). The surprise here is that those who were theoretically guarding our visual heritage were themselves so much under the influence of modernist taboos against history, and were so much influenced by contemporary definitions of what is "creative," that they failed to see how unsympathetic the choice really was.

Superficial attempts to relate are obvious: the new building maintains the cornice line of the old, has the same floor to ceiling and window heights, uses the same material and emphasizes the lower floors as do the old townhouses with their stoops and bay windows. In other words it does everything it can to "line up" with what is already there. But this favorite intellectual approach often ends, as it does here, with a visually unsatisfactory product. And for specific reasons.

The 19th century townhouses nearby are completed compositions: each has a stoop, bay window with paired windows above and is finished by a decorative cornice. The new building follows the modern fashion in which the facade is part of a continuum. In terms of composition, it is anchored by the tower on the corner, but it is coincidental that it stops where it does on the right. Without the older buildings it could go on forever. It is vertically uncomposed as well. Arbitrarily cut off, without the visual punctuation of an ornamental cornice, it looks naked next to its finished-off neighbors. The new facade is conceived in the modern idiom, as the corner of some enormous abstract pattern that could extend infinitely in two directions. The designer's formula-happy efforts to build a correspondence here are just not enough to convince the unconscious wisdom of the eye.

Jehovah's Witnesses Building, Brooklyn Heights, New York: Ulrich Franzen Associates (1970).

Detail of Jehovah's Witnesses Building showing adjoining houses.

Danieli Excelsior Hotel, Venice

In talking about fitting new with old, the visual complexity of the context invariably comes up. What if there is "no context"? That is, what if there is no easily recognizable and reasonably homogeneous style to follow? I would point out, as we have seen from the previous example, that mere homogeneity of context is no guarantee of an easy fit. The Danieli Excelsior Hotel is more successful in its circumstances than the Jehovah's Witnesses Building, even though its architect was confronted by a more visually varied, less easily pigeon-holed context. That it fits in so well is particularly interesting as it does so while breaking a number of the more generally accepted rules.

The Danieli, for instance, has a different number of floors from either of the adjoining buildings; also the proportion of window to solid wall is different, and its window proportions also differ from those of either neighbor. There are subtle alignments, however, that contribute to its success, among them its role as a step between the building on the left and the Danieli Hotel on the right. But the most helpful elements are the balcony railings and the ornament at the cornice line which echo those of the older building. The newer version is more severe, to be sure, but the relationship would be considerably less convincing without this fine scale detail.

Addition to the Boston Public Library, Boston (Philip Johnson, 1976.)

The Boston Library addition demonstrates that even when a majority of high priority criteria are met, success is not automatic. The addition uses the same stone as the original Library, maintains the same cornice height and horizontal divisions, and even emulates the arch motif of the old entrance, although this is done at a difficult scale. Yet with all this effort, there is still a feeling of discontinuity. It becomes clear when we look at the facade treatments, that this is due mainly to the new building's lack of appropriate detail.

Danieli Excelsior Hotel, Venice (date unknown).

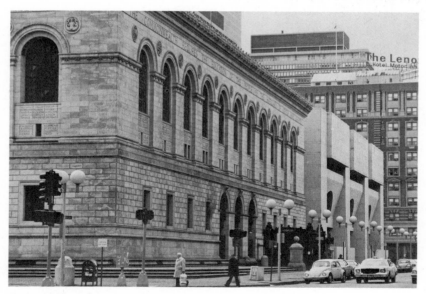

Boston Public Library; McKim, Mead and White (1887) and
Addition; Philip Johnson (1971).

Although the addition uses the same limestone as the original, the differences in the way the stone is used are stronger than any connections due to similarity in color. The surface of the old Library is alternately smooth and rusticated, with prominent moldings and string course, producing a rich visual texture. The addition has a uniformly flat surface throughout, relieved only by the faint pattern of the joints.

Detail of Boston Public Library.

Alternative detail of Boston Public Library. (Photomontage: Angus Macdonald.)

The way the two buildings meet the sky is the most striking demonstration of the futility of blind rule-following even in a good cause. From a distance the two roof lines are similar. However, the roof slopes, while visible from a considerable distance, disappear when seen from across the street. Thus the passer by, and the actual user of the library sees only the upper edges of the facades. McKim, Mead and White understood its visual importance and enlivened the potentially boring edge with an ornamental treatment derived from classical motifs. The Johnson addition, with its enslavement to the gods of simplicity, leaves us with an awkward bluntness, all the more marked by inevitable contrast with the grace of the earlier building.

Longy Music School, Cambridge, Massachusetts (Huygens & Tappe, 1971.)

The solidity of the old masonry is virtually caricatured by the blank brick. It captures none of the visual flavor and is particularly disturbing where the roofline meets the sky.

C&A Department Store, Amersfoort, Holland (ca. 1960s.)

The town fathers of Amersfoort insisted that the C&A Store erected in the 1960s should fit comfortably in the old town's center. The design was disastrous, however well intentioned, because it did not go far enough. The new storefront does use traditional materials, its long facade is appropriately divided into vertical proportions, and its gables, however insipid, are reminiscent of traditional forms. There are, in fact, only a few dissimilarities: its windows are a slightly different proportion; the arcaded ground floor is atypical and, of course, there is minimal ornament. Unfortunately, the facade is stultifyingly regular, capturing none of the variety that exists in the rest of the street. It screams out its alien modern presence next to the rich mixture of neighboring stores: anonymity versus individuality, predictability versus variety.

Longy Music School, Cambridge, Massachusetts; Huygens & Tappe (1971).

C&A Department Store, Amersfoort, Holland (ca. 1960s).

The alternative design for this Dutch street adds a "group" of background buildings to a streetscape composed of background buildings. (Photomontage: Angus Macdonald.)

Townhouse, Society Hill, Philadelphia (ca. 1960s.)

Here again some of the major design criteria are doggedly followed, to no avail: the cornice height is maintained; the same material is used; the floor heights are the same; even the proportions of the doorway and the second floor window are virtually the same as those of the older houses. But the nature of the traditional townhouse facade composition has been fatally altered, not to speak of the general dullness that reigns here because broad manipulations of large areas have been substituted for more visually interesting, small scale articulation.

Addition to the Portsmouth Library, Portsmouth, New Hampshire (Stahl-Bennett, 1975.)

The architect of this addition has said that it had to take this form because of "new programmatic requirements." Yet all he has done is to put these "new" requirements into a simple box. It could have been decorated with any type of ornament or fitted with any type of window and still have accommodated, as has the "parent" building, the functions of a library.

Whether or not a building suits its purpose is seldom if ever affected by elements of style. Nevertheless, function continues to be used as an excuse for contrasting with the existing context, when the real reasons are more likely to be aesthetic or ideological prejudices.

Townhouse, Society Hill section of Philadelphia (ca. 1960s).

Portsmouth Library and Addition, Portsmouth, New Hampshire. Original building by Charles Bulfinch (1806), addition by Stahl-Bennett (1975).

Detail of Portsmouth Library and Addition.

Warwick Cresent, London
(date unknown.)

Here are two groups of houses, one in the modern style, the other traditional. Neither is an extraordinary example of its kind. Their juxtaposition, however, shows the inherent poverty of certain principles of modern design and how difficult it is to follow them and still make an architecture that is hospitable to the human spirit.

The older houses make a strong rhythm as their bold elements advance and retreat from the streetline. Their decoration is eye catching, but not overly rich, and proves essential in defining the units' progression. These houses unite to form a dignified composition along the street.

The modern flats around the corner are pathetic by comparison. Their identical color scheme explicitly says that they would like to be related, but their overall statement is only a caricature of the old, reducing the size of the elements, accelerating their movement and destroying the grace of its rhythm. The pieces are too small; there is no boldness or generosity in their movement, only agitation. A stately promenade of ladies and gentlemen turns the corner and becomes a production line of identical parts, an endless row moving indifferently towards an unknown destination. The eye does not follow along pleasurably, but hurries down the crescent just to be done with it. This is hardly the makings of great townscape.

Westborn Terrace, London (date unknown).

Westborn Terrace and Warwick Cresent (dates unknown).

Another choice for Warwick Cresent would be to acknowledge the more dignified rhythm of the early row. (Photomontage: Brent C. Brolin.)

70

800 Fifth Avenue, New York City
(Ulrich Franzen Assocs., 1978)

In discussing his re-design of a developer's facade for a Fifth Avenue apartment building, Ulrich Franzen gave an important insight into why his earlier Jehovah's Witnesses Building failed to relate sympathetically to its neighbors. He also illuminated the emotional and technical problems which designers now face when trying to fit their buildings into ornamented surroundings.

When he accepted the commission, Franzen said, he decided that the new building should have an ornamental facade if it was to relate graciously to its neighbors, including the refined Hotel Pierre to the south, and the neo-Georgian Knickerbocker Club to the north, both designated landmarks. He told me that he had even thought of finding an old facade stored away someplace that might be grafted onto the new frame. None was found, and the new facade, while a good effort, suffers from the anemia that afflicts so many other modern attempts, and for the same reasons.

The tentative, abstracted neo-classical decoration of this building seems to be the result of two things: a basic timidity about designing with ornament, probably engendered by spartan modernist training, and the lack of skills required to invent or to design with it even if one wanted to. The architect admitted to me with refreshing candor that neither he nor anyone in his office had the skills to design with ornament. These are predicaments which all too many architects now face.

Bank Building, Campo Manin, Venice

Irregularities and tendencies towards the picturesque characterize Italian towns and their piazzas. This rather uninteresting building is made much less disturbing than it might have been because of certain irregularities, some of which come from its siting and others from small variations within its own, basically regular facade.

Because of its siting we see only about three-fourths of the building's front. This has the fortuitous consequence of making the symmetri-

cal facade appear asymmetrical relative to the Campo. A full front view, with its pediments and bland facade grid entirely visible, would certainly have dampened the lively tone set by the other buildings around the Campo.

A closer look shows that the balconies too do not line up properly with the pediments; they are one bay short. (Note the bays with deeper shadows.) This adds visual tension because the eye expects regularity yet senses the difference.

These irregularities help but are not enough to keep Campo Manin from suffering unnecessarily from a dull, repetitious intrusion.

800 Fifth Ave. , New York City, Ulrich Franzen Associates (1978).

Bank Building, Campo Manin, Venice (date unknown).

Townhouse, West 11th Street, New York City (Hardy Holzman Pfeiffer, 1979.)

A few years ago the explosion of what was alleged to be an ammunition cache belonging to an underground group, destroyed an old townhouse in Greenwich Village. Although the original 19th century character of the street had not been perfectly preserved, architecturally, it still had a strong visual flavor that the residents recognized and took pleasure in. When it came to replacing the destroyed facade, the architects made an attempt, respected by some critics, to relate the new building to its context by the device of contrasting new and old in the same facade.

The top and ground floors are traditional; there are typical attic windows above, complete with trim, and even a stoop at ground level. The middle floors, on the other hand, have modern fenestration, and the facade plane is pivoted so that it juts out four feet from the wall plane established by the row of seven houses of which it is a part.

The attempt to evoke the image of the older houses is clear in the literal copying of top and bottom floors. The contrasting insertion is, by definition, out of character; it makes no *visual* sense except as a way of pointing out that the building was "architect designed." It is as though the architects had hung a neon sign on the facade to call attention to its creative innovation. As eminent a critic as the New York Times' Ada Louise Huxtable declared the building to be a "brilliant attempt at a synthesis of new and old." The building does not synthesize; it merely juxtaposes, violently. It is as though some child of a mixed marriage had been born with black limbs and a white torso.

The critic goes on to say that, "When the old fabric is gone, it cannot be brought back." This is patently not true, if one remembers that fully eighty percent of the handsomest old buildings in the U.S. today must be described as neo-georgian, neo-gothic, neo-classic, etc. The only possible explanation for such an untenable claim is the lingering modernist feeling that it is sinful to imitate. (The Romantic's equation of art with originality still dominates our thinking, threatening anyone who "imitates" with certain excommunication from the body of True Artists.) The simple materials and techniques needed to build a facade as it might have looked in 1840 are found, with little difficulty, today. (See Prete House, page 146.) Such a facade would possibly have cost even less than the new design, considering the increased window area, the expense of the cantilever and the waterproofing problems in the recessed, rain-catching area.

It is equally fatuous to argue that such a jarring facade is symbolically important because it reminds the residents of the tragic bomb blast that originally cleared the site. Local residents will not soon forget that explosion and interested tourists would probably prefer to read details from a plaque, rather than try to decipher this typically obscure elitist iconography.

When a new building is to be fitted into a neighborhood with such a strong visual character the best solution is often—and was surely in this case—to design as though you were working in that period. This does not necessarily mean copying the blown-up facade literally, but suggests working in the formal language of that era, with an eye towards relating the facade to its immediate neighbors. As we saw in the historical examples, there can be considerable leeway in such an approach, depending only on the skill and ingenuity of the designer. (See conclusion, page 142 for further discussion of the alternatives.)

Townhouse, West 11th Street, Greenwich Village, New York
City; Hardy, Holzman Pfeiffer (1979).

More Successful Examples

In my view, the following examples relate to their respective contexts relatively successfully. The reasons for this vary. Some are better at doing it than others. Some are more beautiful in the way they succeed. But the more beautiful buildings are not necessarily the more successful at fitting in. A building which is beautiful by itself may become less than beautiful when it is placed in a context which it does not respect.

Each one of the following examples is interesting for the ways in which it makes these connections, including a number notable for breaking rules that are normally considered important in establishing a sympathetic relationship.

Elliot House, Chevy Chase, Maryland
(Hugh Newell Jacobsen, 1976.)

This is an exquisitely complex statement of the present design quandry encompassing all our contradictory feelings about originality and fitting in. The right side of this house is old; the left side is a recently completed copy of part of the older house. They are joined by the familiar glass link. But something is strange, because this link usually connects new with old. Here it is the only modern element in sight.

The addition is an exact copy, on the exterior. The link between them is literally an "equals" sign. Therefore, although it reproduces the old to the let-

Detail of "link" between new (left) and old; Elliot House, Chevy Chase, Maryland; Hugh Newell Jacobsen (1976).

Overall view of Elliot House.

ter, it does not exactly *look* old. That is to say, an addition that copies its parent *precisely* is the exception rather than the rule among old buildings. This forces us to do a double-take because what we see is different from what we would expect of a "normal" builder's addition to a conventional house. A builder wanting to make a compatible addition would probably follow the original detailing fairly closely but vary the general shapes, as in the Nantucket House (see page 31). This would result in a new wing that resembles the old but which does not necessarily equate itself with it as this one does. It would have been a true add-ition.

The new wing is not only an attractive addition, it is, intentionally or not, an eloquent philosophical statement which subtly draws attention to itself and makes the following statement about our predicament: It is visually wrong to build a modernist addition here but we are not yet comfortable enough with history, or with the apparent sacrifice of the designer's ego, to playfully invent from the old forms and produce something that would blend almost invisibly with the original. It should be noted here that many "uneducated" builders and carpenters routinely design and build such compatible additions. But they are unencumbered by modernist ideology.

The glass link confirms that the architect did not want his addition to blend in to the point of becoming an undifferentiable part of a whole. It is the typically honest, modern gesture giving away what would otherwise have been an intolerably dishonest deception. It lets us in on the secret; something is new here, the game is to guess what.

Green Hall, Columbia University, New York City (Robert Stern, 1977.)

Breaking up large surfaces with moldings to create a more intimate scale and to relate a renovation more closely to the style of the existing building is virtually a lost art. In this lounge at the Columbia University Law School, Robert Stern practices this craft once again with considerable success.

The moldings' symmetry gives a sense of appropriate formality. The placement of the main panels at the springline of the arch lowers the apparent height of the room and makes it seem more intimate. The entire interior gives one the impression of being both old and new.

Green Hall, Columbia University, New York City, Robert Stern (1977). (Photo: Ed Stoecklein.)

Butterfield House (center), New York City; Mayer, Whittlesey & Glass (1962).

Butterfield House, New York City (Whittlesly & Glass, 1962.)

This apartment was placed on a street which already had a mixture of styles and building types. Yet it still seems to fit well. The reasons for this are obscure at first, but after some looking one discovers that its balconies and those on the taller building are what make the connection. This is surprising, as they are different on each building. The older building's ornate ironwork balconies are stuck onto its flat front; those of the newer building are hollowed out of its facade. Nevertheless, the resulting shadows—below the older and above the newer balconies—solidify the relationship because they create a similar pattern: Different means achieve the same end.

Addition, Martha's Vinyard, Massachusetts (Armstrong Childs Assocs., 1978.)

This is a pleasantly awkward addition, a bit comic in a friendly, carnival-pavillion-like way which goes well with the feeling of the original tower and house. It has a flavor all its own but its frame construction, pitched roof, and color make it clearly a part of the whole composition.

NEW

Two views of an addition to a house on Martha's Vinyard,
Massachusetts; Armstrong Childs Assocs. (1978).

6

New Buildings with Neighborhood or Regional Styles

Less Successful Examples

Goldman Salatsch House (Loos House), Vienna (Adolph Loos, 1911.)

The Goldman Salatsch Building, by Adolf Loos, caused quite a stir when it was completed in 1911. It was one of the first buildings to intentionally contrast modern and traditional styles and can still be seen opposite the Hofburgh on Michaelerplatz. One contemporary reviewer attacked its lack of ornament as "blatantly dissonant modernism," saying that ". . . from the lowest point of the threshold to the bridge tiles of the roof, there isn't a trace of anything Viennese . . ."

Loos replied to this criticism with an argument that was to become standard with modernists. He declared that though he was harmonizing with the 18th and 19th century buildings around the square, he chose to relate to them *indirectly* by recalling the simpler building tradition of medieval Vienna (although no such examples existed on the Plaza). He side-stepped the actual surroundings to make a reference to something no longer a part of the nearby scene.

This more abstract, intellectual approach—rather than taking a cue from the existing immediate visual context—often occurs in modernism. While an ideologically tenable argument, it is often visually weak. It can succeed only if it creates a strong visual symbol that transcends the context and does not become entangled in petty visual feuds. If the eye is disturbed by its lack of visual continuity, the mind will not be able to dwell on the meaning of the symbol. From the present vantage point Loos House seems too weak to establish a convincing bridge between the medieval past and the later buildings. The only way to shore it up is with specific visual reinforcements: a representative medieval building that is near enough to make a *visual* connection.

Coming back to Loos House, after the decades of visual destruction wrought by modernism, it is a bit difficult to understand why the building caused such an uproar. It seems almost benign. It keeps the same horizontal divisions as the adjoining buildings and even has a top, a simple cornice and mansard roof. Both are bold concessions to history that later modernists would not dare to risk. Even the natural veining of the green marble on the lower floors has its own strong if "honest" decoration that alludes to its more elaborate neighbors. Only the strident change in color and the self-conscious nakedness of the upper floors reminds us that this building was a harbinger of even more hostile incursions to come.

Goldman Salatsch House (center), Vienna; Adolf Loos (1911).

Hofburg, Imperial Palace of the Hapsburgs, located directly
across the Michaelerplatz from Loos House. The Emperor
Franz-Josef was one of those most offended by this "contrast"
of new and old.

Brunswick Center, London
(Patrick Hodgkin, 1974.)

The extreme horizontality and technological exhibitionism of this glassy monster of a ziggurat make it seem threatening to the traditional buildings around it. It seems poised, ready to crash ahead wiping out a great swath of the city on its way. This is particularly clear when you are in the trough between the two banks of apartments. Such a violent change in form (as opposed to materials, as we will see in the next examples) is, almost without fail, a visually fatal blow.

Two views of Brunswick Center, London; Patrick Hodgkinson (1974).

House and Offices, Amsterdam, Holland
(Abel Cahen, 1971.)

This attempt is moderately successful, primarily because of its compatible scale. The asymetrical top is less disturbing than it might have been because from most angles it is not so noticeable.

Other aspects are more jarring. The choice of materials detracts because of its ugliness compared with the traditional brick. Concrete weathers poorly under the best conditions and the northern climate has already made this look slummy. This is particularly disturbing when we see that it has been faced with brick where the new building meets its neighbors. One regrets that this appropriate gesture was not continued; if it had been, the lack of trim and peculiar window shapes would have seemed less foreign.

Apartment and office building, Amsterdam; Abel Cahen (1971). Detail of top.

Street view of Amsterdam apartment and office building.

Store Fronts, Upper East Side, New York City, (dates
unknown).

Woolworth Store, Oxford, England, and East Side Storefronts, New York City

These two examples would seem to indicate that the form of a building is more important in relation to its context than the materials it uses. The overbearing monolithic form of the Woolworth Store destroys the potential for connection attempted by its random courses of local fieldstone, a sympathetic traditional material. The traditional details of the New York City storefronts, on the other hand, beautifully if surprisingly crafted in stainless steel, make them compatible with the general character of the other stores in the area. Form dominates; there is no need for similar materials.

Blackwell's Music Shop, Oxford, England (Gillespie, Kidd & Coia, 1970.)

The roofline of this shop has the pleasant quality of seeming old or new, depending on your frame of mind when you see it. The recessed entrance is less fortunate. Apparently local officials did not want the appearance of further commercial encroachment on this predominantly residential street, ruling out another traditional storefront. The result was something more disturbing than a modest continuation of the store on the left; a new and unrelated element in what had been a relatively uncomplicated street.

Blackwell's Music Shop, Oxford; Gillespie, Kidd & Coia (1970).

Woolworth Store, Cornmarket Street, Oxford. (date unknown).

(Left) U. S. Embassy, Grosvenor Square, London; Eero
Saarinen (1960).

Neo-Georgian building adjoining U.S. Embassy, Grosvenor
Square, London.

U.S. Embassy, London (Eero Saarinen, 1960.)

Eero Saarinen was unique among modernists in the clarity of his design responses to each new situation. The U.S. Embassy, on Grosvernor Square in London, is a good example of his method. It is not strictly successful in the terms of this study but we should bear in mind that it was designed decades ago, when establishing a sympathetic relationship to the context was not one of the criteria used in judging architectural talent.

Saarinen cues on two elements of adjoining buildings: the accented window frames and a pronounced dentil course running the length of the north side of the Square. In the Embassy facade the traditional frames become a large concrete checkerboard and the dentil course a crinkly parapet.

The Embassy's gray color is somewhat dreary for predominantly red- and orange-bricked Grosvernor Square and one could wish that Saarinen had been more sensitive to this. But the building deserves attention and should appeal to the more conventional modernists for the inventiveness of its connections.

Had Saarinen lived long enough to develop this design approach I feel sure that, for those concerned with context, he would have been the most important architect of this half-century.

Lee Burns House, Los Angeles, California (Charles Moore, 1974.)

An article in *Progressive Architecture* (4:75) declared that this house has a strong affinity to the Spanish Colonial architectural style commonly associated with Southern California. This opinion reflects the casual criteria that are still acceptable when confronting the question of fitting new with old.

The alleged relationship to the regional, tile and adobe style fails to materialize, even with the most sympathetic eye. The colors of the new house make the main contribution, recalling the earth-tones of Spanish tiles shading white-washed adobe—although here the walls are colored and the roof is white. To my eye, beyond that tenuous connection, the house lacks a convincing sense of the regional style. There is no pretense to adobe solidity here, and that is one of the strongest characteristics of the regional style. The windows look as if they were cut out with a matknife. Indeed, this is one of the cardboard houses of the sixties and it literally looks like the chipboard models from which it undoubtedly evolved. There is little reminder of traditional massing either. This is a direct descendant of the shed style of which Charles Moore is an acknowledged master, with his customary wood or shingle siding exchanged for delicate tints that warm in the afternoon light.

All this makes it a lovely place to be, but has little to do with the familiar regional style. The modest bungalow in the lower left of the second photograph is immensely more successful with its simple tile roof and tiny verandah.

Lee Burns House, Los Angeles, California; Charles Moore (1974).

Lee Burns House and "California style" bungalow (date
unknown).

Faculty Club, University of California, Santa Barbara (Moore & Turnbull, 1968.)

The Faculty Club at U.C.S.B. presents a similar situation. It is an interesting building, a sort of self-contained Italian hilltown, but one does not sense the mission-variety California style it supposedly recalls. That is the style of the Santa Barbara County Courthouse and of many other buildings in downtown Santa Barbara, which were rebuilt after the earthquake of 1925 and which borrowed freely from the regional style. This rebuilding was an enormously successful experiment in creating a unified townscape, as Charles Moore himself has pointed out.

The comparison between the Faculty Club and the Courthouse presents an interesting problem regarding the relationship of a new building to its regional context. In *The Place of Houses* (p. 20), Moore and co-author Don Lyndon say that the visual coherence of a town like Santa Barbara is not created "just by 'style,' by white walls, tile roofs and black wrought-iron grilles. It is fundamentally created by a characteristic relationship between people and enclosure." While it is best to have both, I would say that the element of "style" is by far the more important of the two. Abstracting the relationship between people and architecture in this way—emphasizing generalities rather than

specifics—is distinctly reminiscent of the modernist viewpoint that de-emphasizes the importance of ornament in maintaining the character of a place. The authors go on to describe how, in Santa Barbara, the general relationship between architecture and people is created by open-roofed courtyards and the changing light and shade which one experiences when walking from open to arcaded spaces.

The Faculty Club follows this line of reasoning in that it has the "bones" of the local style—in its courtyards and covered walkways—but not its

Faculty Club, U.C.S.B.

Faculty Club at University of California, Santa Barbara; Moore and Turnbull (1968).

Santa Barbara County Court House; William Mooser (1929).

El Paseo, a shopping street in Santa Barbara; James Osborne Craig (1925).

"clothing," the ornamental details. There are no arches, no orange tiles peeking over the eaves, no column capitals, no wrought-iron railings. The relationship between these two buildings and the regional style to which they are both supposed to allude goes a long way to prove, to my eye, that it is the details which actually do most to create the flavor of the "places" about which Moore and Lyndon speak. The Faculty Club is a neutered building; its flavor is not rich and specific like that of the Courthouse. It would be at home in any number of "places." The Courthouse has definite links to the local architectural past which simple generic attributes like enclosed courtyards and covered passageways cannot begin to evoke by themselves. On the other hand, while the "clothing" may create a truer sense of place, it alone, without an understanding of the "bones," is also unsatisfactory.

Courtyard of the Faculty Club, U.C.S.B. and alternative with ornament. (Photomontage: Angus Macdonald.)

Lang House, Connecticut
(Stern & Hagmann, 1974.)

Architects often feel they can design with a freer hand if they build where there is no man-made context. Though it might seem that there can be no contextual restraints if there is no architectural context, the situation is not always so. I visited the Lang House and, knowing it from color photographs, I was prepared for what I was to see: an Italianate, yellow-stucco-like house sitting on a hillside at the edge of an open field. Because it is relatively isolated I had hardly expected to notice that the house did not have any sort of "New England" look to it. Nevertheless, when I saw it from a distance I could not erase the cumulative visual memory of the villages and farmhouses I had passed during the half-hour drive through the countryside from the main highway. Although it stood alone I had the uncomfortable feeling that this strange Italianate house was out of place in Connecticut's rolling hills.

Addition to the Claghorn House, Princeton, New Jersey
(Michael Graves, 1974.)

The as yet timid advances towards history in post-modernist architecture demonstrate two things: traditional modernist morality still inhibits designers, and obscure historical references do little to enhance a contextual relationship. This modest addition is a classic example.

The original clapboard house was built in the 1870s. It is a typical builder's house of that time, with casual details like the gable front, diminutive Doric porch columns and decorated moldings which make diluted yet unmistakable references to the classical past.

Lang House, Connecticut; Stern and Hagmann (1974).

Claghorn House, Princeton, New Jersey, front (ca. 1880).

The addition is probably best described as a cubist collage. With the exception of bits of molding and lattice work, there are no historical references that would make it understandable to anyone not familiar with the architect's personal iconography. Actually, the symbols employed here have more of a literary than visual connection to the old house. The architect has said that, as certain parts of the original house derive from classical Greek architecture—the pediment and porch columns, for example—the new addition can relate to the old house by returning to the same Greek precedents. So it is poly-chromed, as were Greek temples, and a four-sided [sic] shape is put over the kitchen window to recall half a classical pediment. The other half is found to the right, over the doorway leading from the small patio to the dining room. The relationship between these fragments is virtually impossible to see when standing in front of the addition; one has the distinct feeling that it was more convincing in two dimensions, as it was conceived than, it is in three. Other allusions are equally strained.

While the architect's obliqueness may come from an intellectually defensible sophistication, it might also grow out of a common fear of contemporary architects that borrowing too literally opens them to the charge of "copying" rather than "creating."

Mr. Graves has said that one should be able to appreciate architecture on several levels as one does, for example, a novel of James Joyce. It is nice, although not imperative, that architecture have multiple layers of meaning; if it does, however, the first and presumably most literal layer should at least be comprehensible. "Ulysses" may be a maze of literary allusions but it is also comprehensible on a more immediate level. If the simplest meanings are obscure there may not be sufficient interest to penetrate the more esoteric ones.

Taking inspiration more directly from the old house would have resulted in a more visually appropriate, if less noticeable, addition. But modernists, or the new eclectics as they have been been called, are sometimes a peculiar breed. They often declare that they will once again make architecture comprehensible to a broader public by using popular, historical allusions, and then throw away the opportunity by ignoring the most obvious and insistent history, already in front of their eyes.

Rear of Claghorn House, showing addition by Michael Graves (1974).

More Successful Examples

Trubeck & Wislocki Houses, Nantucket Island, Massachusetts (Venturi & Rauch, 1971–72.)

These summer cottages do not copy the traditional Nantucket style. They do not have, for example, the white trim which characterizes most of the island's architecture. They are also considerably larger than the tiny and often ancient fishing cottages of the nearby village of 'Sconset. Yet these newcomers have some of the same feeling as their elders.

The apparent casualness of their fenestration helps. There seems to be some degree of accident involved; it does not look as though they had been self-consciously "designed" as in most modern houses, although I am sure they were. The traditional shingles also help make a connection.

The simple shape of the houses is another interesting factor because it is *not* like that of the older cottages which grew, with additions, over many years. The Venturi and Rauch cottages are not additive but are complete units with their peaked roofs and porches. In this sense they are almost archetypes. But within the archetype the architects have captured the individuality and home-made-over-the-years quality that typifies so many of the island's houses. Among other things the apparent bulk of these two-story houses has been skillfully reduced to make them more like the other older and smaller cottages. Note the size of the double window in the side of the far cottage. When first seen from a distance one takes it for a normal-sized residential window. Only later do we realize that it is closer to one and a half times larger than we had thought. However the expectation is that it is smaller and so we adjust the rest of the house accordingly, making it, too, seem smaller than it actually is.

The porch steps are similarly deceptive. Experience tells us that three steps is not high; we know that a step is about 6" to 8" high, so three of them add up to about 1 1/2 feet. But look closely at the concrete block next to the steps. (Concrete blocks are 8 inches high.) We see immediately that the stair riser has been constructed nearer 12 inches rather than 6 inches high, making the porch floor nearly three feet above ground. Our eye, which "wants" to see another diminutive Nantucket cottage, has been fooled. From a distance it saw the steps as smaller than they actually are, and our mind's eye adjusted our perception of the house to fit what we thought of the steps and windows. Presto, the house shrinks to the size of the tinier ones we are accustomed to seeing.

Trubeck and Wislocki Houses, Nantucket; Venturi & Rauch (1971–72).

Fishing cottage, Sconset, Nantucket (ca. 18th–19th centuries.)

This manipulation is particularly interesting when we realize that these cottages are among the few two-story buildings on the island outside of Nantucket Town.

Shopping Center, Water Mill, New York (Peter Paul Muller, 1977.)

This is unembarrassed historicism, but without the awkwardness that sometimes accompanies more literal attempts which try to stretch a traditional vocabulary over a set of inappropriate new shapes.

This is the sort of "sacrilegiousness" that makes modernists cry; a so-called fake style in concrete block covered with clapboard—double dishonesty! But it *works* in the visual context of Water Mill, Long Island. And it is certainly more welcome than some jarring modern "statement".

Shopping Center, Water Mill, New York (1977).

Apartment House near Vercelli, Italy (1973.)

This large building evokes, with some success, the feeling of Italian villages which have been formed by years of accretions. Like its historical predecessors, it seems both homogeneous and diverse, because it recycles the same themes—in form, color and ornament—but never in boring or repetitive ways. In fact, few architectural groupings are used more than once. The part of the building nearest the camera, for example, hints at symmetry, but little deviations here and there continually throw it off track.

Office Building and International Seaman's House, Savannah, Georgia (John Lebey, ca. 1965.)

The form and materials of this historical-looking building are traditional; the fenestration is contemporary. The result is an unfortunate mix. While it might possibly be acceptable in another city, Savannah has such a strong historical flavor, so many authentically old and distinguished buildings, that this sort of pastiche tends to look mannered, even cheap.

The better choice was probably John Lebey's more specifically historical International Seaman's Home, built in 1965. It is built of concrete block finished with tabby, a mixture of lime and water, with local seashells for aggregate. The main building (on the left) and smaller chapel make a beautiful modulation from the historical house on the right, around the corner to the square, even though the rounded arch windows of the Chapel and the end of the Seaman's House are almost totally different from those of the older house. The massing, porches and other fenestration of these buildings make them so at home in Savannah that the casual passerby would scarcely notice that they were newly built.

Apartment House near Vercelli, Italy (1973).

International Seaman's House, Savannah, Georgia; John Lebey (ca. 1965).

Commercial building, Savannah, Georgia (ca. 1960s).

International Seaman's House, Savannah, Georgia.

Brant House, Bermuda
(Venturi & Rauch, 1977.)

This clever intellectualized architectural parody seems like any one of a number of other large Bermudian houses, but only at first glance. Its typically traditional ornamental entrance pediment recalls the grand days of the "great house," while its additive massing makes it look as if it surely had been built over many decades rather than in 1977.

Then one begins to notice the splendid peculiarities. Instead of using a decorative motif consistently, the architects have played variations on a theme: only one part of the house has quoins at the corners, and on closer look these are not even real quoins, but a visual shorthand recalling the original. A high, round window lets in the southern light; it is a fairly common device, but this particular window opens into a relatively small space and is the size one would expect to find on a medium-sized Renaissance church. The seaside arcade, accidentally on purpose, lines up neither with the doors and windows behind it nor the verandah columns above. Other island homes of comparable pretension make sure that their arcades and fenestration conform in an orderly manner. The verandah above this arcade has two-dimensional cutout columns with so much entasis that they become cartoon characters; one cannot take them too seriously because they have literally been cut out and pasted on.

Entrance (from land side), Brant House, Bermuda; Venturi & Rauch (1977).

TRADITIONAL DECORATIVE PEDIMENT

"QUOINS"

Brant House, Bermuda; cartoon quoins and oversized round window.

TRADITIONAL QUOINS

Modest Bermudian house showing the traditional form of the quoins.

Brant House, Bermuda; lower arcade which does not align with doorways behind. Note the flat, cartoon columns of verandah above.

Brant House, Bermuda; seaside verandah with paste-on cartoon columns.

Our brief discussion here cannot touch on all the strange and witty things about this house that the attentive eye eventually discovers but the oddities are intentional and rooted in the Bermudian architectural idiom. The "joke" of this house, if joke is not too blunt a term for a sophisticated play on architectural elements, is that everything is a bit wrong but, as a whole, it still looks peculiarly Bermudian. It is not a slavish modern copy—pseudo Bermuda—but instead is a literate architectural essay, fooling the casual onlooker, yet leaving something rewarding for the closer observer to discover. It is firmly anchored in local building tradition yet makes a decidedly unique, contemporary statement.

Paget Hall, Hamilton, Bermuda (ca. 1930s).

Leidse Spaarbank and Addition, Leiden, Holland (1877; 1975)

The original building was built in 1877. The addition is interesting because it borrows quite literally some elements from its parent and invents intriguing variations on others.

The ground floor lintels have been borrowed, but simplified. The "tower" railing is repeated with only a slight change (its ballusters are set back from the railing edge) as the cornice element of the addition. The corbeled brickwork below the new railing is without precedent, although it picks up the rhythm of the four narrow arched windows above. This is an agreeable combination of eclecticism and invention.

Leidse Spaarbank, Leiden, Holland; (left) 1877, (right) 1975.

Houses, Colmar, France

Here again is an example to confound the rulemakers, a good rhythmic and proportional relationship exists between new and old even though the new houses utilize a fundamentally different construction, and initiate what should be a fatal change in the character of the wall. Instead of traditional rectangular windows punched out of the bearing wall, the new walls are all windows, stretching the full width of the houses; the traditional bearing wall structure is changed to column and beam construction. However, in this case the radical difference is overcome by several factors.

The new houses have roughly the same massing, rooflines and materials as the old, and their balconies echo the traditional horizontal spaces between window lines. As we have seen in a number of previous examples, however, such elements are no guarantee of a workable relationship (see the Strasbourg Houses, page 104 and the Jehovah's Witnesses Building, page 63).

One specific further circumstance allows the mix to work so well: the curving street turns the new facades slightly away from their older neighbors. This change in orientation separates them into two visual groups although they are actually one con-

Four new houses on an old street in Colmar, France (dates unknown).

tinuous row. They seem to be farther apart than they really are, which makes the dissimilarities of wall and window less disturbing and allows the combination of other sympathetic connections to carry off the marriage.

Townhouses Opposite Pompidou Center, Paris (ca. 1970s.)

One would think that the overlapping planes of the partial curtain walls of these houses would be too out of character. Their windows, also, are not the "correct" proportions and even the roof windows—not true dormers—are different from those of the neighboring townhouses to the right.

But there is just enough variety in the roof treatment to be interesting rather than discordant, while the design of the facades emphasizing the vertical rather than horizontal axis gives them a sense of variety within given limits that exists all along the streetfront. A nice example of a similar visual character created through the use of a different architectural vocabulary.

New Housing, Chartres, France

This relatively large building nevertheless maintains an appropriately small scale, blending well with its neighbors in the medieval village of Chartres. It is helped by the chimneys and two types of dormers which break up the massive rooflines. But the key is the fenestration; not only is it irregular, better reflecting the character of the older buildings, but its irregularity is achieved by using what we must assume is a cost-effective variety of combinations of three basic window types in a peculiarly modern, almost mass-production way.

Townhouses opposite Pompidou Center, Paris (ca. 1970s).

New Housing, Chartres, France (ca. 1960s).

Gamma Building, Leiden, Holland
(M. P. Schutte, 1973–74.)

This new building occupies several lot widths. The local solution for a building of this size has been to cover it with one big roof, as we can see from the example of the older building on the right, setting it apart from the choppier rhythm of the single-lot houses. The Gamma Building has combined both modes; it is a large building which is broken up so as not to overwhelm its smaller neighbors. In this sense it is a hybrid, a newly forged link between the two older building styles.

Slight changes in the facade plane divide it into narrower vertical sections sympathetic to the traditional proportions of the smaller houses. The height could have proven a problem, as it is over half again as high as the smaller houses on the left. The roofline has been broken up, however, in a way which continues the variety of the street. It not only echoes the horizontal cornices and sloped roofs of the others but utilizes a white trim, particularly at ground level, which connects the building even more surely to its context.

Gamma Building, Leiden, Holland.

Gamma Building, Leiden, Holland; Architecten Bureau, Ir. M. P. Schutte (1973–74).

Graben #16, Vienna (ca. 1930.)

Some early 20th century "modern" architecture was noticeably different from the historical styles yet retained a sensitivity towards its traditional surroundings, something hard core modernism never tolerated. This Art Deco building in Vienna is perfectly at ease beside its historicizing 19th century neighbor although the former has nothing that is recognizably historical about it. It fits in simply because its architect invented visually compatible variations on its neighbor's ornamental themes.

The older building emphasizes the corner by a gentle rounding and discreet change in wall plane; the newer one also rounds the corner but emphasizes it differently, with a tower. The Art Deco building does not copy the older corner rustication literally but adopts rustication-like abstractions with horizontal lines only. It has a straight-line silhouette but keeps our interest at the skyline with false cornices and an ornamental frieze below the eave, accomplishing the same purpose as the see-through ballustrade on the older building.

This invented ornament creates a sympathetic visual texture. It does simplify somewhat, and in that way could be considered in the modern tradition, but it retains considerable small scale detail in contrast to the familiar broad-brush contemporary approach which bores the eye by wiping out all intimate detail.

Graben #16, Vienna (ca. 1930).

Ausonia Housing for the Elderly, Boston; Garufo/Roberts
(1977).

Ausonia Housing for The Elderly, Boston (Garufo/Roberts, 1977.)

It is possible to design a building that respects the context and is also a magnum opus. Few modern examples exist, although I have shown several from the past. In this era of self-centered architectural "statements" it is far more courageous, and no less demanding in skill, to recognize the need for and to design a background building.

This is what Garufo/Roberts Associates did, in the Ausonian Housing, working with a neighborhood citizen's group (The Waterfront Restudy Committee). It is one of those rare contemporary works that truly blends into its surroundings.

The four and five story brick houses nearby are from the 18th and 19th centuries. Their ground floors are accented by white granite columns and massive lintels. The Ausonia connects with them in several ways. It repeats the ground floor trim, but in concrete, and with longer spans. Although it is one large building (the photograph shows only half of it) the Ausonia's facade is divided by recesses in the brickwork into panels that echo the quicker rhythm of the older three-bay fronts down the street. The windows within these panels are not arranged traditionally, but the proportions of the smaller ones are similar. And they keep the original bearing wall character.

The old buildings have an irregular skyline, because they are different heights. The Ausonia matches their variety by cutting away some parts of the top floors to make roof terraces with lower parapet walls.

Houses Near The Ponte Vecchio, Florence (Post World War II.)

Few visitors are aware that these buildings are new. The original Renaissance houses were destroyed during World War II. The replacements show characteristic Italian skill and concern for the street, or in this case the river, ensemble. Only by looking carefully does one notice that the facades are unabashedly modern, so cleverly do they reflect the massing and rhythm of past centuries, blending graciously with the older houses that jostle one another on the south bank of the Arno.

Houses near the Ponte Vecchio, Florence (post World War II).

Streetscape, Strasbourg, France

This agreeable street scene composed harmoniously of a modern and an ancient side, is interesting because it works, as do many of the more successful examples, by breaking the accepted rules for evolving compatible design.

While these new buildings do have the same number of stories as most of the old, their floor-to-ceiling height is substantially greater; in some cases nearly half again as high as the old houses. What is more, the new buildings are all the same height, whereas the old ones vary from three to five stories. The plane of the new facades is also broken up—sometimes cantilevered over the first floor—while that of the older houses maintains the street line strictly from base to cornice. Finally, the new buildings are uniformly white, starkly accented with darker window frames, string courses and roofs, while the older ones are white, gray, brown, beige and other shades, with nondescript detailing.

There are some similarities. The windows of both old and new are cut out of the facades in a manner characteristic of bearing wall construction. Some windows of the new buildings also have traditional painted frames, and the whole is capped with a small eave overhang and dormers. But the major discrepancies—increased, almost dominating height, strictly maintained eave height, a single color, and the regular interruption of the facade plane—seem near-impossible obstacles to overcome. Why then, do these elements contribute rather than detract?

The list of design criteria that we discussed earlier was, of course, compiled on the assumption and the hope that it could constitute a generally applicable system; that there are certain high ranking items, such as maintaining cornice height and street lines, that are untouchable. Tamper with them and the relationship will fail. In our actual sampling, however, it becomes uncomfortably clear that few, if any, principles are really sacred. With skillful juggling, one can compensate for the omission of almost any apparently essential elements.

New and old apartment houses, Strasbourg, France (ca. 1970).

Furthermore it is not necessary to use exactly the same forms or details to attain the same visual impact; there are usually several architectural ways to make a facade busy or calm, directional or non-directional, grand or personal. To return to our Strasbourg *rue*, we can see that the old facades form a continuous wall along the street, while their rooflines, being of different heights, make an irregular silhouette. There is another complication; each old house shifts slightly to follow the curve of the street, which lends even more variety to the skyline.

The new buildings, even though the economics of modern construction dictate that they be all the same height, have a similarly irregular roofline. The designer has here found another way to achieve this comfortably random characteristic by extending alternate bays over the ground floor so that, when seen from below, they make evocative irregularities in the eave line.

The subtlety of this solution is particularly evident when we look at a less successful overstatement of the same intent in some even more recent buildings around the corner.

The feeling of the street changes sharply with the newest facades. One feels lectured to. Although their roof shape is similar, their upper floors jut out as do those of the other building and their windows are approximately the same proportions, there is a radical change in the surface appearance and therefore the total effect of the facade. Instead of looking like a bearing wall, the designer chose to have it express (to use the popular word) the column and beam structure. Thus, the spaces between the windows get smaller and we begin to read them as narrow "columns" rather than as parts of the larger structural plane, called the "wall." The recesses below the windows then become insubstantial in-fill panels rather than a solid part of a bearing wall.

The self-conscious balcony treatment also contradicts the feeling of the bearing wall. Rather than being shallowly cantilevered as they are in the other new building, they thrust into the street, held in place by eye-catching slabs set at right angles to the wall.

Even with the close similarities in height, material, color, scale and roof shape, these slight changes in the character of the wall, attention grabbers, essentially, interrupt the sense of continuity. While to the professional this interruption may seem reasonable, there is a footnote to this analysis—the layperson's point of view. While I was taking these photographs the foreman of a workcrew renovating one of the old buildings started talking to me. When I asked him which of the two new groups of buildings fit better with the old he pointed, without hesitation, to the first of these two examples.

New and newer apartment houses, Strasbourg, France.

New Housing, Zwolle, Holland
(Aldo van Eyck, 1977.)

This group of modern flats is well integrated into the traditional streetscape. The group faces the town on three sides and also forms an interior garden court and street of its own. One notices the sympathetic elements immediately. The houses are built out of the traditional brick; their facades are traditionally proportioned and they meet the sky with a modern version of the rather more elegant old curved pediment (visible over the new roofs). Windows are arranged asymetrically, in the modern fashion, but retain the traditional bearing wall character. There are other minor deviations, such as the arches over the small upper floor balconies, but, as in traditional Dutch houses, the ratio of window to wall is high, giving the interiors a soft Vermeer-like light, while their verticality echoes that of the older fenestration.

The direct connection from street to apartment interior is also typical. Even bedroom windows facing onto the street have sills not more than 30" above the floor. This would be insufficient to give a sense of privacy in the U.S., but is in keeping with what constitutes an acceptable relationship between public and private spaces here.

The gardens attached to the houses facing the court are still another traditional arrangement. In Weissenhof, the modern housing settlement in Stuttgart (1927), the Dutch architect J. J. P. Oud provided similar traditional gardens for his spartan modern flats.

New housing, Zwolle, Holland; Aldo van Eyck (1977) and old.

Van Eyck's houses offer variations on the theme of the surroundings yet, within their limits, they are rather repetitive. This too is familiar, recalling the uniformity of much traditional Dutch housing. The only lapse in this orchestration is the lack of white trim. Van Eyck uses red, which tends to recede when seen with the traditional white trim.

All things considered it is a pleasure to see such humanly scaled, visually appropriate modern housing.

New and old housing, Zwolle.

Housing over parking, Zwolle.

View from ground floor apartment, Zwolle.

New and old housing, Zwolle.

Saganaw Avenue Mural, Cambridge, Massachusetts (Jeff Oberdorfer and local residents, Cambridge Arts Council, Sponsor, 1976.)

This is one of the more amusing, least honest, and perhaps oldest ways of changing an indifferent setting into an appropriate one: disguise it with painting. The Italians are masters at this. It has worked wonders on dull, box-like German Baroque buildings, and here, on a supermarket wall in Cambridge, Massachusetts, where it breathes life into the dead ending of this residential street.

Star Market wall, Cambridge, Massachusetts (at end of Saganaw Avenue).

Painted interior, Church of the Coronation, Sabbioneta, Italy (1586).

Saganaw Avenue Mural, Cambridge, Massachusetts; design: Jeff Oberdorfer, painted by local residents with materials contributed by Star Market, Cambridge Arts Council, Sponsor (1976).

7

New Buildings with Older Landmarks

Less Successful Examples

Addition to the Metropolitan Museum of Art, New York City (Roche, Dinkeloo, Assocs., 1979.)

Contrasting old and new often results in meaningless departures from the existing context. This addition to the Metropolitan makes a perfunctory attempt to relate to the old McKim, Mead and White building by using the same facing material (the base) and by its roughly similar height. But the relationship would still appear purely accidental were it not for the typical modern connective gesture of despair, the reveal.

(Right) South Wing of the Metropolitan Museum of Art, New York City (1906) McKim, Mead and White. (Left) Addition to house the Michael C. Rockefeller Collection of Primitive Art, Roche, Dinkeloo & Assoc. (1979).

Wintertur Insurance Company and the Karlskirche, by Fischer von Erlach (1737), Vienna.

Alternative design for Wintertur Insurance Company. (Photomontage: Angus Macdonald.)

Alternative design for Wintertur Insurance Company. (Photomontage: Angus Macdonald.)

Wintertur Insurance Company & The Karlskirche, Vienna (ca. 1960s; Fischer von Erlach, 1737.)

Here is the legacy of Adolf Loos' attitude. Architectural confrontations such as this are fatuously referred to as "contrasts between new and old" and are commonly justified to an incredulous public as being economical and practical. The photomontages show three possible alternatives which use the same plan, materials and construction techniques, but relate to the Karlskirche with considerably more grace.

East Wing of The National Gallery of Art, Washington, D.C. (I. M. Pei, Assocs., 1978.)

The new East Wing offers an example of the problems which can occur when a doctrinaire modernist must relate his design to an existing context. This addition was required to conform to the main building, in height and exterior material, in order to establish a sympathetic relationship. The intent was only partially realized—and even this limited success seems to have been achieved in spite of, rather than because of, the architect's other choices.

Alternative design for Wintertur Insurance Company. (Photomontage: Angus Macdonald.)

The East Wing is avowedly modernist, and conveys the aim of that philosophy: to create a personal architectural statement, devoid of historical references, which may be seen as a symbol of our times.

There is a profound and irreconcilable conflict between this ideological aim and the intent behind the rules specifying height and materials: the former encourages a unique artistic expression; the latter hones for an aesthetic synthesis.

The desire for personal expression in the East Wing overwhelms the counter-demand for synthesis. Although the addition is really an addendum to the main gallery, it calls attention to itself like a petulant child. A tiny building, on a tiny site, it is sliced into more angles, and has more dramatic height changes, than all the other buildings on the Mall, put together. It stops just short of neon signs to announce its presence.

This is the modernist statement *par excellence:* the physical embodiment of the architect's ego. It is an outsized piece of sculpture which arrogantly—even disrespectfully—competes with the vastly more important Capitol Building, when seen from the west, and with the National Gallery, when seen from the east.

While the addition was forced to take on some characteristics of the parent building, its modern style permitted none of the subtleties of scale which enhance the National Gallery. When faced with the visual problem of large, blank exterior walls, for example, John Russel Pope responded by mak-

East Wing of the National Gallery of Art, Washington, D.C.;
I. M. Pei (1978).

National Gallery of Art, Washington, D.C.; John Russel Pope (1941).

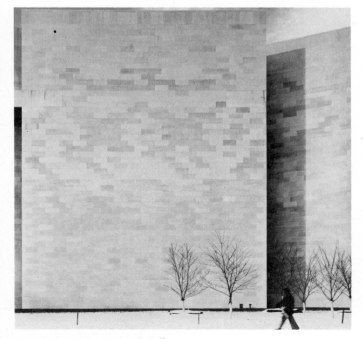

East Wing of the National Gallery.

ing them into stately compositions, through the careful use of moldings and changes in wall plane. These refinements assure that the walls will be as interesting when seen from a distance as they are from close-up. The East Wing, on the other hand, presents us with absolutely blank walls (some of them one-hundred and ten feet high!) which are appallingly dull. The sole respite from boredom is the faint pattern of masonry joints. One can only imagine that this building was conceived in miniature, and then enlarged to its present size without considering how our perceptions of it would change as its size increased.

An architecture critic has pointed out an interesting similarity between these two neighbors. The original neo-classical Gallery, completed in 1941, was a conservative building for its time. I. M. Pei's addition too "does not stand at the advance (architectural) guard" but also tries to do the best it can within what is now recognized as the conservative modern style. This is an accurate observation, but it does not go far enough. The original Gallery was conservative for a reason; at the time it was built Washington's major buildings were almost all neo-classical, although modernism had been a world movement for nearly twenty years. By working within that conservative style, the architect was acknowledging the primacy of the city's character over the claims of a new architectural fashion.

The conservatism of the present addition is a far less positive gesture, coming simply from an ideological posture unsympathetic to any but the most fleeting references to its surroundings.

To design a good, or even great, modern building for this site would solve only half the problem. Ironically, the addition might well have been more sympathetic to its parent building had it been designed by one of the less conservative contemporary architects. The present avant-garde—those who want to bring identifiable history back to architecture—might have had better luck in making the needed connection.

House, Savannah, Georgia (T. Jerry Lominack, 1973.)

This house shows the casualness—or unsureness—with which design criteria are now applied. It was completed in 1973 and, as a part of the Troup Ward Urban Renewal Project in Savannah, was subject to design criteria requiring it to establish a sympathetic relationship to its neighbors. *It was seen as satisfying these criteria!*

The architect himself describes the house as an attempt to fit "a contemporary structure within the (historic) district." I tried to get further information from him as to how this attempt had been formulated but was unsuccessful. It would appear from the photographs that his theories would have to be quite convincing to dispel the visual problems.

The game of fitting contemporary architecture with old has tended to follow the pattern established by modern painting which Tom Wolfe describes so amusingly in *The Painted Word*. The work of art (or in this case architecture) has become un-understandable without its theory, the words which attempt to convince the mind of what the eye cannot accept.

Modern house in Savannah, Georgia; T. Jerry Lominack (1973).

Modern house in Savannah, Georgia.

Allen Memorial Art Museum (left), Oberlin College; Cass
Gilbert (1917) and Ellen Johnson Gallery of Modern Art, by
Venturi & Rauch (1974).

Bosworth Hall, Oberlin College; Cass Gilbert (1931).

Addition to the Allen Memorial Art Museum, Oberlin College, Oberlin, Ohio (Venturi & Rauch, 1974.)

In his characteristically thoroughgoing manner Robert Venturi conscientiously evolves a firm historical justification for the design and style of his own recent addition to the original Allen Memorial Art Museum, by Cass Gilbert (1917). He postulates two fundamental aspects of Gilbert's design theory which appear in several buildings at Oberlin. First, both "plain" and "fancy" styles are employed in the same buildings and, second, there is always a distinct contrast between the front and the back of each building.

These two principles are both connected to the establishment of a hierarchy of forms while at the same time maintaining the unity of the whole. The separation into a hierarchy is explicit in the idea of "plain and fancy" and "contrast" between front and back. Integration is implicit in the idea of a whole building composed of parts of greater and lesser importance.

Bosworth Hall, Oberlin's School of Theology (1931), is the building most closely analogous to the Museum and its new addition, and this is the Gilbert building to which Venturi devotes the most space in an article discussing his addition in the Bulletin of the Oberlin Art Museum, (Vol. XXXIV, No. 2, 1976–77, pp. 83–104).

The main wing of Bosworth Hall, containing classrooms and a chapel, is built of fancy buff limestone in a modern Romanesque revival style. Behind it is a less important dormitory wing in plain brick with modest detailing although, as Venturi points out, it has "vaguely Romanesque articulation in the brick." By holding to the principles he identified in Gilbert's work, Venturi implies that he has linked his addition to the Museum and, in the larger sense, to the architectural traditions established by Gilbert at Oberlin. With this in mind, let us look closely at the Museum with its recent addition.

Front wing of Bosworth Hall.

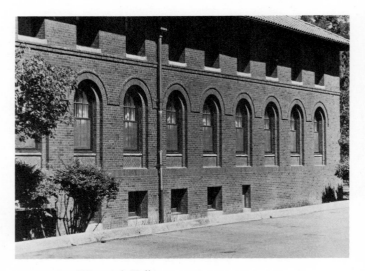

Rear wing of Bosworth Hall.

The Museum's recent addition has two parts, the Ellen Johnson Gallery, which is immediately adjacent to the old building, and a loft space for studios and offices next to that. According to the architect's analysis, the addition conforms to the characteristics of Gilbert's buildings in the following ways: The addition steps back from the main building in jogs, acknowledging its dominance; the addition plays the "plain" to the Museum's "fancy." The flat surface of the new building, while in theoretical harmony with the low relief of the Museum's moldings, also contrasts by appearing "recessive" compared with the Museum's sculptural entrance. In a more "subtle" contrast, the new wing continues the same color scheme and materials as the old—pink granite and rose sandstone—but in a different pattern: a checkerboard versus Renaissance motifs.

The plain and fancy idea is carried through in the new addition itself by opposing the fancy checkerboard of the Gallery to the industrial detailing of the loft.

Corner at which the Ellen Johnson Gallery of Modern Art meets the loft space. Together, the Gallery and the loft space constitute the entire addition.

Detail of Allen Memorial Art Museum and Addition.

NEW

Now that we have heard the explanations, let us look more carefully at how the relationships work visually. Keep in mind that Venturi bases his theories on the degree of *visual connection* between the front and back wings of Bosworth Hall and tries to reevoke this connection between the Museum and his addition to it. Remember that the eye, and not the mind, must be convinced that the respective pairs belong together.

Gilbert's front and back wings of Bosworth Hall, first of all, have closely related visual motifs. Gilbert established the hierarchy in this building by repeating the same forms, front and rear, in different materials. The shapes are repeated while the means of executing them are varied. By isolating each wing we see that both have arched openings on the lower floors, with smaller rectangular openings above. The lower dormitory windows are recessed, like those of the front, and have similar although more modest dripstone moldings. Both wings also have string courses separating upper and lower floors and low tile roofs with generous overhangs. The fact that the forms are repeated in different materials reinforces their similarities.

The Venturi and Rauch addition to the Museum, however, reverses this approach; the formal motifs are changed while the materials remain pretty much the same, at least in the Johnson Gallery which directly abuts the Museum. This constitutes, we are told, a valid intellectual link between the main building and its addition. The question is, does it work visually?

According to the architects, the neutral checkerboard pattern should recede. It does not. In addition, its lack of a clear scale relationship to the older building makes it hang ambiguously behind the delicate Quattrocento moldings. The addition's height does not help; its bright yellow fascia charges aggressively into the receding tile roof.

The architects seem to have made the courageous choice (to use their own expression) of "jamming" the addition up against the Museum rather than using the typical glass link or reveal. By butting directly into the Museum they say they have acknowledged that the transition must be made by the small scale details rather than at the scale of the building's mass. (That is, they have not made the whole building contract at that point to form a reveal.) Ironically, after that bold and unconventional choice they settled on what amounts to a link, but at a smaller scale: a flush, vertical strip of gray granite separating Gilbert's history from their checkerboard by ten inches. Like the allegedly shunned *cliché*, it seems to pretend that the two buildings never meet.

Butting buildings together was commonplace in the past. This is the northwest corner of the Piazza San Marco, Venice. The building on the right was completed 300 years before Napoleon I closed off the Square with the building on the left.

Corner at which the Ellen Johnson Gallery meet the original
Museum. Note the slate "link."

"LINK"

The very clumsiness of this addition—Venturi calls it "inevitably awkward"—inclines us to hazard that Gilbert's principles, as enunciated by Venturi, must just be untrustworthy. And one might yield to this inclination were it not for the proximate example of Bosworth Hall, which succeeds so well using just these same principles, its front and rear wings joined by an arcade which is "awkward" in no one's language.

The fault then lies with Venturi's intellectual assumptions, devoid of traditional common sense about visual continuity, which Gilbert understood.

At this point we should note, with regard to the "inevitability" of its awkwardness, that Venturi and Rauch's was not the first addition to the Oberlin Art Museum. A small wing, creating a courtyard, was added by Clarence Ward, in 1937.

It too followed Gilbert's principles but also held to the building's *visual* logic. As a result, it seems to be an inseparable part of the original design.

In preparing us for their explanation of how the new wing follows in Gilbert's footsteps, the architects said that they went about the design "as a Quattrocento architect might have added to a real villa in Fiesole two generations after it was built; we juxtaposed a workable new block in an architectural style current today." In other words, they chose to add a wing in the "now-modern" style. The ogre here is, of course, the Modern Movement and its penchant for intellectual rather than visual standards. From the examples we have discussed earlier, we can see that adding on in a different, or "modern" style can be done in such a way as to strengthen rather than fragment the whole composition. Venturi's defense of his work simply demonstrates that, in architecture, ideas are no substitute for visual refinement. The eye demands satisfaction on its own terms.

Addition (forming cloister) to the Allen Memorial Art Museum, Oberlin College; Clarence Ward (1937).

The front and rear wings of Bosworth Hall are joined by an arcade.

More Successful Examples

The National Permanent Building and the Old Executive Office Building, Washington, D.C. (Hartman & Cox, 1977; Alfred B. Mullett, 1871–88.)

The National Permanent Building is an interesting essay in accommodation. It comes, perhaps, as close as a completely modernist structure can to capturing the spirit of the Old Executive Office Building's sculptural facade, a few blocks away on Pennsylvania Avenue. It attempts this by exposing its mechanical ducts, which attenuate as they rise, and heading them with stylized capitals and lintels over each bay. The eye recognizes this as a friendly gesture, as it does the suggestion of a mansard roof line. The connection is predictably strained at close range because of the new building's lack of detail, but the intent is welcome and the execution interesting.

The National Permanent Building, Washington, D.C.; Hartman and Cox (1977).

Detail of Old Executive Office Building.

Detail of National Permanent Building.

Old Executive Office Building, Washington, D.C.; Alfred B. Mullett (1871–88).

Addition to Quincy Market, Boston, (Benjamin Thompson, 1976.)

Quincy Market's addition offers an example of successful contrast of modern and old, particularly on the exterior. The original building is a blocky, austere Greek Revival structure with virtually no exterior ornament. In this sense it is well-attuned to modern taste. To this the architects have attached two transparent cages of black steel and glass. These are a total departure in color, material and proportion of window to wall—the additions are all window, no wall—from the original building.

Addition to Quincy Market, Boston, Massachusetts. Original building by Alexander Parris (1824–26); addition by Benjamin Thompson (1976).

Addition to Quincy Market, showing portico column.

Interior of Quincy Market Addition.

Yet in spite of these major differences the additions fit well because their visual character is similar to that of Quincy Market: both are taut, linear and severe. The shadows cast by the window reveals in the masonry wall make a linear pattern like that of the thin steel members of the addition; the second story spandrels give much the same effect.

The height and width of the addition are respectfully proportioned with regard to the main building; its roof slope also approximates the angle of the entrance portico closely enough to suggest the relationship without being trite.

These additions work dramatically because they are subservient—leaning against the mother building in an unthreatening way—and because their linear, severe character is very much like that of the original.

The clear relationship between stern Doric Revival and hard glass and steel is muddied a bit in the interior by a seemingly perverse attack of honesty: all of the glass building's innards, whether new wiring or old brick sub-structure, are proudly displayed. The contrast might work better if fewer things were so "honestly" shown, so that we did not lose track of the sense of old structure and new services in a visual jumble.

Addition to The Frick Collection, New York City (Van Dyke, 1977.)

This wing is virtual perfection as addition to an already monumental composition. In fact it would take an expert to tell where the old ends and the new begins. Yet it is not a "copy," in that the details are not duplicates of the existing, but elegant variations on the themes present in the original Frick mansion.

The usual architects' claim that such a building costs much more than one done in a more modern style is put to rest here. In fact, the addition to the National Gallery in Washington, D.C., which we discussed earlier, cost 22% more per square foot than this one ($156/s.f. versus $128/s.f.!).

Interior of Addition to Frick Collection.

Addition to Frick Collection, New York City; Harry van Dyke, in association with John Barrington Bayley & G. Frederick Poehler (1977).

124

8

Large Buildings with Small Buildings

Two Buildings, Venice

Similar, but not identical details are important in connecting these two buildings. The one on the left is an architectural footnote to the larger building, a poorer relative that is different in scale and color but still convincingly related. The awnings help considerably. The middle floors of each building have windows with elaborated frames; there are fan windows over those on the right and blind panels on the left. All of the openings have trim; a simple stone frame in one case and appropriately more serious archivolts, capitals and so on in the other. Finally, the formal ballustrade of the roof is faintly echoed by a wiggle of tile-ends, peeking over a delicate reminder of a cornice.

Two buildings, Venice (dates unknown).

The Massie School, Savannah, Georgia (John Norris, 1855–86.)

The original building (in the center) was completed in 1856; the additions to the right and left came in 1872 and 1886 respectively. The ensemble maintains the scale of the other buildings around this Savannah square by repeating a small element three times instead of increasing the bulk of the one each time it needed enlarging. The original school building has a different scale and detailing; yet its tripartite mini-monumentality brings it close enough to the feeling of the row houses to be a quite friendly neighbor.

Openbar Library, Amsterdam, Holland (De Klerk, 1977.)

There are apparent similarities between old and new here: the new buildings use the same material, they have similar trim, their roofline is irregular and their proportions approximate those of narrow, older buildings on either side. But these are not new buildings, they are *one* new building which the architect has broken up to blend with the residential scale of the street. This way of fragmenting the facade is not traditional. Older buildings butt into one another directly. These four pseudo-independent facades never touch. They are separated by glass reveals. The ground floor of this four-in-one building also disregards the upper divisions and cuts across them in a distinctly untraditional way. And the asymmetry of its windows also ignores the past.

The Massie School, Savannah, Georgia; John Norris (1855–86).

In spite of these notable differences the traditional shapes of these floating facades make a strong enough connection to their context to counteract the discrepancies. Some people will undoubtedly be disturbed because this one building sneakily pretends to be four. But predictability in buildings, as in people, may not always be a virtue.

The most serious weakness is its lack of a strong conclusion at the cornice. Overall, however, it is a skillful example of a larger building being scaled down to fit, almost unnoticed, into a street of residentially scaled neighbors. (This is, of course, only one way to solve this problem. Another is to make a monument which, by definition, need not pay too close attention to the surroundings.)

Openbar Library, Amsterdam.

Openbar Library, Amsterdam; De Klerk (1977).

Townhouse, Park Avenue, New York City (Robert Stern, 1975.)

This small Park Avenue townhouse sits in midblock between much larger buildings of mixed architectural antecedents, in what many would call a nondescript context. Nevertheless, a thoughtful designer has found recurring themes and used them as connecting threads. For example, the surrounding buildings have the traditional, three-part division of bottom (somewhat fancy), middle (rather plain), and top (again, somewhat fancy). They also have moldings, pilasters and string courses that are, loosely speaking, "classical."

The townhouse, sometimes too discreetly, picks up on these themes to make visual connections. Its mid-section has pilasters on either side that rest on a cushioned base, the horizontal band about three feet above the top of the doors. Their small, projecting capitals appear to support a weakly defined entablature—another classical reference—which is actually the entire upper floor.

While the ornament seems timid, particularly at the skyline, it is a bold gesture for our spartan times and is effective where it appears. It is most successful over the street-level doors, where it is most defined, and least effective at the top where the "entablature" has no strong visual conclusion.

The building seems dated in the best sense, as though it had been there for some time, yet belonging to our time as well.

Townhouse, Park Avenue, New York City; Robert Stern (1975).

Detail, Townhouse, Park Avenue, New York City.

Townhouse, Park Avenue, New York City.

New Executive Office Building, Washington, D.C. (Warnecke, 1968.)

The mansard roof of the New Executive Office Building on Jackson Place was a good choice, particularly in relation to the old Renwick Gallery around the corner. With trim, it might have been less ponderous; however the main problem is that the huge bulk of this building is overbearing, even threatening when seen from Jackson Place. It would have been a more successful "background" building had its mass been more broken up, so that it looked like several smaller buildings. This viewpoint is substantiated when we move around the corner and see it over the Renwick Gallery. Here the unrelieved massing of the Jackson Place facade changes; its huge hulk is broken into three smaller, more manageable pieces which make it less overbearing.

New Executive Office Building, Washington, D.C.; John Carl Warnecke (1968). Seen from Lafayette Park.

New Executive Office Building, seen from Pennsylvania Avenue, over the Renwick Gallery.

Detail of Dodge Center, Georgetown, Washington, D.C.; Hartmann and Cox (1976).

130

Dodge Center, Georgetown, Washington, D.C. (Hartmann & Cox, 1976.)

This new commercial building is interesting because the nature of its relationship to the context varies considerably depending upon one's vantage point. It is most successful when seen from close by, at the street level. One is more aware of the compatible height of its street facade and less aware of the enormous bulk behind. On the whole it is a satisfactory solution viewed from the street.

It helps our understanding of the problem of placing large buildings among small ones to look at nearby older commercial warehouses that are as large as this building but which maintain a sympathetic relationship to their smaller neighbors.

When seen from a distance, we sense the Moise Safdiesque, megastructural forebearers of the new building and the residential ancestors of the older ones. The new building is only one small segment of what could be a grandiose urban-scale structure. It represents one small part of a grander concept. The older warehouse is merely an enlargement of a simple residential idea, a bigger version of the houses in the neighborhood.

Distant view of Dodge Center and its neighbors.

131

The Torre Valasca, Milan (Belgiojoso, Peressutti, Rogers, 1958.)

The ultimate extension of the Dodge Center situation is Milan's famous Torre Valasca, where the scale is wildly out of balance. The twenty-story tower broods over the cityscape of adjoining buildings which are at best only five or six stories high. Yet there is an agreeable sense of organic continuity because the Tower successfully captures the character of the historical buildings around it despite its modern materials and exaggerated form.

Torre Valasca, Milan; Belgiojoso, Peressutti, Rogers (1958).

Similar Contexts: Bruges, Belgium, and Rotterdam, Holland

Traditional and modern approaches to the same problem: fitting a relatively large building into a smaller streetscape. Although the modern building in Rotterdam looks much larger than its neighbors, it is actually less than twice their height. The building in Bruges is also tall, relative to its neighbors on the left. But the modern one *seems* much bigger because its style is so drastically different. To see how similar the two situations actually are, the ratios of small to large facades are: Bruges, 1:1.6; Rotterdam, 1:1.8. By comparison, the Recorder's House, in Bruges (page 24) was less than half as high as the Town Hall, the actual ratio being 1:2.2.

The modern building is well-designed in its own right, using the reveal, like a giant foot, to push the old buildings away and give itself breathing room. However, it is an unconvincing gesture; the new building remains very much *with* its neighbors, no matter how vehemently it denies the community. For all the pretense towards honesty in modernism, this building, like many others, dissembles by pretending to be alone. The self-delusion is disturbing because, in refusing to acknowledge the older buildings, it strikes a fatal blow to the dignity of the street. It is the architectural equivalent of shunting the grandparents off into an old folk's home. Ignoring the problem does not mean it ceases to be.

The Bruges example is more successful because, in spite of its different style, its decoration and detailing help to maintain the scale and character of the street. This building stands there, like a rich cousin, somewhat pompous but definitely related. The Rotterdam building is indifferent, almost insolent.

Street, Bruges, Belgium.

Street, Rotterdam, Holland.

Economist Buildings, London
(Smithsons, 1966–68.)

It should be almost impossible to establish a compatible relationship between modern skyscrapers and smaller buildings, although the Smithson's 1968 Economist Buildings are interesting on several counts because of their relative success.

First of all, the tallest building has been tactfully set back from the street. Their surface texture, if ultimately dull because of its repetitiveness, does make a gesture towards evoking the feeling of the neighbors' more elegant detailing. More importantly, the beveled corners, an echo of the building to the south on St. James Street, are inherently passive forms, making the complex less aggressive than it would have been with the standard right-angle corners. The buildings are least successful at close range where their lack of imaginative detail is most noticeable.

Economist Buildings, London.

Economist Buildings, London; Alison and Peter Smithson (1966–68).

Hancock Tower, Boston (I. M. Pei Assocs., 1973.)

The architects of Hancock Tower faced the preposterous problem of putting a sixty story building on the corner of Copley Square without overwhelming both the square and its focal point, Richardson's Trinity Church. They approached it with tact and skill notably lacking in their addition to the National Gallery five years later. The tower could not bring off this miracle entirely, but it is remarkable how little it intrudes upon the historic church and Copley Square.

Two things are responsible for this relative success. Its mirror-glass curtain wall almost makes the building disappear when you look up at the tower, and, of course, it reflects Richardson's magnificent church below.

The tower's trapezoidal plan is a less obvious but even greater help. Standing near the church, the tower becomes a giant, two-dimensional false-front. This is because its second side, the one that would ordinarily be visible, falls away because of the acute angle at the right hand corner. While the tower still dominates because of its staggering height, this two-dimensional aspect diminishes its presence sufficiently to preserve the ground-level dominance of the church.

When you walk far enough away from Trinity to see the other side of the tower, it still stays less disturbing than one might expect, as its bulk seems to pull back and away, in deference to the church.

Hancock Tower, Boston; I. M. Pei Assocs. (1973).

Hancock Tower, Boston.

This sketch shows how bad it could have been had the tower wall not been set obliquely. (Photomontage: Brent C. Brolin.)

Delft, Cathedral Square, Holland (1384–1496).

9

Monuments

The monument—whether civic, religious, corporate, academic or otherwise—presents the one clear situation in which *contrasting* with the existing architectural context is always an acceptable choice.

Cathedral Square, Delft, Holland

The giant Cathedral faces the Town Hall across a square flanked by burghers' houses.

Church, Mayfair, London

A mini-monument; this species need not be large to contrast.

Guggenheim Museum, New York City (Frank Lloyd Wright, 1959.)

The Guggenheim corkscrew is set off by the staid limestone facades of Fifth Avenue.

Church, Mayfair, London. The mini-monument.

Guggenheim Museum, New York City; Frank Lloyd Wright (1959).

10

Conclusion

Since the late 1960s a growing number of architects have begun to question the rules of modernism, to move beyond their restrictions towards new interpretations of their craft and art. In doing this they have acknowledged the importance of the general historical context; they have recognized what the general public knew all along, that historical associations in architecture are important. But too often they make random references with no meaningful connection to the immediate surroundings. These architects seek to become a part of the grander History of Architecture, but they ignore the simple visual facts forming the context in which their new building will be seen. (The examples of Stern & Hagmann's Lang House and Michael Graves' Claghorn addition come to mind here, page 89.) The next step, then, is to recognize that the *specific* context too is a valid, even an essential source of design inspiration.

Ego

There are several almost insurmountable obstacles to this simple decision to encourage visual continuity in architectural design. The most prominent of these is the architect's ego. Early in their training, young architects learn to design buildings that stand out from their surroundings, that are readily identifiable as "architect-designed." This is the entrenched contemporary ideal of creativity. (It is also a good way to establish a reputation; if a building is not highly visible, who will know it was architect-designed?) Few stars of the profession are in the habit of designing background buildings. On the contrary, as in the 11th Street townhouse (page 72), the new building often seems to hold out a banner announcing its prestigious presence.

I have spoken of the 19th century Romantic origins of this need for personal expression—the affirmation that genius is at work—at the expense of the context itself. This is inextricably tied to the present, unnecessarily narrow definition of architectural creativity: given our present state of mind, architects find it difficult to feel creatively fulfilled if their buildings blend, even gracefully, into their surroundings.

Our present definition of artistic originality and the idea of fitting new architecture with old are like oil and water. To respect the dignity of a neighborhood by designing a new building that fits so well that it is not easily identified as new is incompatible with the view that originality is the prime measure of the artist's ability. If a building blends in too well now, it is assumed that the architect was just not very inventive. He is more likely to be thought of as a hack and a copier who did not have ideas of his own, and so was reduced to composing variations on borrowed themes—as Michelangelo did in San Lorenzo, and Christopher Wren did in Oxford.

The contemporary teaching and practice of architecture encourage this myopic definition of personal creativity, focussing on that spark of genius which supposedly resides in the soul of every architect. The majority of architects are not geniuses, but they are, in all probability, conscientious designers of moderate talent. Perhaps one or two a generation are truly exceptional. Yet we inspire everyone to proceed as though he or she was one of these rare creators, rather than encouraging them to make civilized, soundly designed buildings that help establish a sense of visual continuity in the community. As a result, too many of today's architects feel that they will somehow prostitute themselves if they build anything less than unique in form or concept.

This is no small matter, for it is difficult to overstate the disastrous consequences that forty years of this mode of thinking has had for our cities. It has been argued that design restrictions nip the pure genius in the bud. I would argue that the truly inventive designer delights in surmounting limitations; constraints disturb only those less sure of their talent, whose inner resources are meager.

The architect's responsibility is notably different from that of other artists. Paintings hang in museums; people can choose whether or not they want to see them. Architecture intrudes, without invitation, everyone's daily life. The simple, if admittedly naive solution to this conflict between respectful design and personal expression is to change the definition of a "creative architectural statement" to mean a building which, among other things, also fits gracefully into its context. De-emphasize the cruder variety of creativity— originality through novelty— and stress refinement within the aesthetic confines of the given visual context, whether it is modern or traditional.

Architects who want to blend their work sympathetically into an existing context often find it difficult to do these days, not because they lack the craft, and not even because they are unfamiliar with the visual characteristics of other styles. These things can be learned relatively easily. The problem is more like "writer's block." It is a psychological inhibition rooted in our present definition of creativity.

Do We Need Another "Style of Our Times"?

Another danger is that we once again settle for the idea of an architectural style of our times. In the first place the "our" in this phrase has always been selective; it has meant the architect and those few who shared or paid for the implementation of his aesthetic values. The meaningful architectural symbols of "our times" are surely different for the farmer, the astronaut, and the architect. Secondly, it is clear from what we see around us that the visual problems of our cities and suburbs are ones of cohesiveness and continuity. We should go beyond the idea of one style for our times to a variety of appropriate styles for different contexts. Respecting the spirit of the times is a less valid architectural concept than *respecting the spirit of the place*.

This does not mean, and has never meant, that a neighborhood cannot change. Nor does it mean a simple-minded revival of historical styles—a return to Grecian porticos or Victorian eclecticism. In actuality, while some 19th century eclectic buildings did respect their contexts, more often than not that kind of eclecticism rigidly declared a particular style appropriate to a particular use—Classical for banks, Gothic for churches, Queen Anne for country cottages—without considering the context.

I do not therefore suggest an arbitrary, intellectualized eclecticism which chooses a style without reference to the surroundings, but a more visually oriented *affinitive seeing* to guide designer's choices; a way of designing which would reinforce the character of a neighborhood because its inspiration would be taken from *the spirit of the place*. History has shown that different architectural styles can evolve compatibly and still retain their own unique aesthetic character; this requires only an intelligent, sensitive appraisal of the visual cues of the context and designers who use their craft to create responsive buildings. Whether this is done by rote copying or by the wildest new architectural inventions should not be the concern. "Family resemblance" is what counts; the eye should feel that a congenial presence has been added.

Capturing this family resemblance is particularly difficult when the designer is limited to the vocabulary of modernism. Modern forms are a product of an ideology which aggressively opposes integrating new buildings into existing architectural contexts. Do not be duped by defenders of ill-fitting architecture who say it looks that way because it is "of our times." If it is built today, outhouse or commercial palace, it is of our times and expresses some facet of contemporary life. No single group can successfully define "our" times for everyone.

Persisting Taboos Against Affinitive Seeing

Several other contemporary attitudes impede the progress towards a more sympathetic and effective contextual design. One of them, a direct legacy of modernism, is the fear of borrowing from older architectural forms. It leads even the most respected critics to speak apologetically about architects who are now beginning to link their work to the history of architecture. The critics patronizingly assure us that this is not "simple eclecticism" but a more esoteric (and presumably, therefore, more valuable) excursion into the meaning of cultural symbols.

The reinterpretation of earlier architectural forms is a true and organic way to respect the context; all pre-modernist architecture indulged in it to some extent. Ponder the progression of the Corinthian Capital from Classical Greece, through Medieval Europe and the Renaissance, to Art Deco in this century; there were always new interpretations, but each, in its own way, retained a flavor of the past. Only in our century has this approach been rejected.

Yet some borrowing of forms or motifs is inevitable if a new building is to be securely linked to

its neighbors. The connection can be made in several ways:

-Closely copying the existing design motifs: Frick Museum Addition. (See page 124.)
-Using basically similar forms but rearranging them: Brant House, Bermuda. (See page 94.)
-Inventing new forms which have the same visual effect as the old: Quincy Market, Boston. (See page 122.)
-Abstracting the original forms: National Permanent Building, Washington, D.C. (See page 120.)

The degree to which the original forms are abstracted obviously affects their recognizability. The more abstract, the more difficult it is to connect them to their source. Make them too abstract and recognition becomes impossible. The Claghorne addition (page 89) and the National Permanent Building (page 120) represent different degrees of abstraction. The connections have become hopelessly obscure in the Claghorne addition, while the other simplifies the earlier forms yet retains a clear resemblance. The degree to which one can depart from the original and still keep this family resemblance depends on the skill of the designer.

Post-Modernism and Fitting New with Old

Architects and writers on post-modernism are beginning to see that history is, once again, a legitimate source of inspiration. There is a spectrum of opinion, of course, as to why this is a good idea. As I mentioned in the introduction, Robert Stern states outright that one reason is to relate the building to its context. The more commonly held idea, judging from a number of post-modern buildings, is that stated by Charles Jencks in *The Language of Post-Modern Architecture*. It has a subtly different intention from that which Stern suggests and which I have proposed.*

---

* See: "Post Script," in *New Directions in American Architecture*, by Stern (Braziller, 1977); "In Context, I and II," *Urban Design*, Spring 1977 and Winter 1977–78 and *The Failure of Modern Architecture*, Van Nostrand Reinhold, 1976, by Brent C. Brolin.

Jencks' "radical eclecticism" seems precariously close to the pursuit of yet another style of our times: "The results," he feels, "as yet are not convincing enough to speak of a *totally new approach and style*" (my emphasis). The implication is that we are, once again, waiting for a new, modern style of our times to take shape before our eyes. The very fact that a recognizable style is expected indicates that the relationship to context will be, at best, a secondary consideration.

Thus far the architecture of post-modernism seems to confirm this—particularly some of the examples which Jencks cites such as the works of Lucien Kroll and Atelier at the University of Louvain. Like the modernists, many post-modernist architects produce "object architecture." In this sense there is little difference between a post-modern style (for all places) and a modern style (for all places). It is only a change in fashion, a shift in architectural hemlines, so to speak.

The Architect as Cheshire Cat

The stress on wit and irony in some post-modern buildings also reveals an understandable uneasiness about venturing into the forbidden world of eclecticism. The cartoon-like cut-out columns and incised quoins of the Brant House, by Venturi & Rauch, gently call our attention to the crucial difference between this Bermudian house and others. They comment on the architect's wish not to disappear completely by designing a house that follows the local customs exactly. It pokes good-natured fun at these traditional elements by casting them in a slightly different mold from the way we would expect to see them.

This tongue-in-cheek aspect is revealing because humor is a way of distancing one's work, of insulating oneself from commitment at a time when the true course of architecture seems less and less sure.

Architects are correct in feeling diffident about such commitment, which requires, after all, stepping off the edge of the known world into the nether regions of architecture. Until quite recently it has been a place where few respected designers cared to tread. It is still unacceptable to the large majority but it is only a matter of time.

In spite of the things which could make post-modernism hostile to compatible contextual design, many of its tendencies are sympathetic. It has begun to bring variety, symbolism and ornament back into architecture. And learning to design in a variety of formal languages is essential to designing sympathetically in different surroundings.

Connecting the architect more closely to the users of his building, by using familiar cultural symbols, is also an essential part of designing for a specific context.

Yet there is also an ominous aspect to the evolution of these ideas. Jencks has said that the important thing about a "language" of architecture is its "message." Once it is felt that ideologies must exist as "preconditions for effective discourse," we are back at the same old Modernist stand. The notion that style, something that should reflect aesthetic choice, must be served up with an ideology is more European than American. It immediately brings to mind the European-bred Modern Movement which tied avant-gardism to leftist politics, a connection which persists in many European schools today.

The link between architecture and ideology is a muddy one at best. Fascists and communists both approved of modern architects and their architecture at different times. Connecting architecture to abstract ideas, with the implication that it can advance them—or even illustrate them so that they can be understood by large numbers of people—seriously overestimates the designer's power. Modernists made this error sixty years ago and perhaps it is about to be made again, by this generation, with regard to so-called post-modern architecture. If so, it will be for the same vain reasons: to infuse an aesthetic movement—a simple but respectable *fashion in architecture*—with weighty connotations so that it will be taken more seriously than if it had to rely on its aesthetic merits alone.

Alternatives

If we imagine a visually harmonious neighborhood and assume the architect wants to respect it, there are two basic choices, with a number of gradations in between.

A Less-Literal Connection to the Context

Many neighborhoods can survive, and even profit, from a mixture of new and old, providing that the new vocabulary sensitively embraces the visual character of the existing context. Inventive adaptation is the most difficult approach, however, because modern prejudices have prevented us from refining our sensitivities to the point where we can first make secure and convincing connections, and then be inventive. Most designers have no difficulty being "inventive." The problem comes when they try to combine this with an equally strong sense of continuity.

A Closer Connection to the Context

A more direct way to integrate new architecture into an existing, visually harmonious context is to use motifs derived more or less directly from the existing style, whether that is late Baroque or Early modern. While present-day designers do not have much difficulty thinking about vaguer, more abstract connections to the context such as the general relationship between the Boston Public Library and its addition, page 64, most find a more literal form of eclecticism unacceptable. It attacks the very basis of what *seems to be* the source of their creative freedom. But the fear of inhibiting creativity by placing restrictions on it reveals a misunderstanding of the nature of design. Architects usually abhor design freedom; they are always looking for and adopting tight aesthetic restrictions.

The present rules governing modernism, and to some extent post-modernism, exclude large areas of the potential sphere of creativity which were accessible to designers in former times, including, notably, "working in the style of." Far from offering new options and giving greater reach to the creative spirit, modern rules restrict designers to one well-trod path. Thumb through the professional journals of recent years and you will see that most modern buildings look very much alike: they rely on the same limited family of simple forms and restrained color and detailing. If they are complicated, it comes from building up small, relatively simple pieces, rather than by the traditional means of embellishing larger forms with finer scale details such as moldings, etc.

In other words, modern designers almost always work under severe aesthetic limitations of their own choosing. The key words here are *of their own choosing*. The problems arise when architects must replace their own aesthetic language with another one, appropriate to the context but not necessarily dear to the architect. This seems to occasion at once a frightening loss of artistic confidence, and the illusion of a loss of creative freedom.

We can overcome this illusion of loss. One way to do it is to re-emphasize in the schools, the *craft* of architecture: the many ways in which space, form, color, texture and line can be combined to evoke emotion. Modernists tied the evocation of these emotions to one set of architectural forms which *they* defined as acceptable to "our" times. If designers learn their craft well, they should be able to bring out this architectural emotion regardless of the vocabulary they use.

Architectural creativity should not be judged, as it has been in the recent past, by the style in which the architect works, but by the skill and subtlety with which his style-vocabulary is used. Ten years ago this would have been impossible in any architecture school in this country. If you designed in any but the modern style you were ridiculed until you came into line. It is now becoming possible.

There is a growing body of designers who would like to break away from modernism's forms but who are either inhibited by its left-over taboos or held back because they were never taught how to invent new ornament or how to use old.

Some architects cite technical advances as the

reason for using the modern forms. This argument doesn't hold water. Technology increases one's pallette; it does not dictate forms. The idiosyncratic shapes of I. M. Pei's addition to the National Gallery in Washington are made with the same materials and many of the same techniques as the neo-classical forms of the main Gallery next door.

Others who oppose a more literal connection still acknowledge that it is difficult to tell the near-copy from the originals after a little weathering.* Does a beautiful street have to become less beautiful when we learn that facades we thought were from the 14th century are actually from the 19th? Is Munich's Marienplatz less attractive because its fine Gothic Town Hall is actually a fine Gothic *Revival* Town Hall? (1908) Are we capable of differentiating between deriving sensual pleasure from a beautiful building—regardless of when it was built—and sheer ideological snobbism?

Encouraging the mind to forcibly contradict the eye like this is a peculiarly self-limiting way to make visual judgments. It is like checking the label before you look at a painting in a museum so you will be sure to know how much to like it. If a building is well constructed and does not offend the eye in its own design or in its relationship to its context, why should we object?

The answer lies in the persistence of modernism's moral criteria for making visual judgments. According to this attitude, a building from 1900 that looks like 1400 is, by definition, dishonest, regardless of how skillfully it is designed and executed. I am far less offended by the friendly act of borrowing from one's neighbors to achieve a more sympathetic relationship than by the truly anti-social act of ignoring them for what is, ultimately, the satisfaction of an individual's ego. With the exception of monuments, I doubt that we can have a truly great urban architecture that is indifferent or hostile to its surroundings.

---

* "True or False: Living Architecture, Old and New," Carl Feiss and Terry B. Morton, *Historic Preservation*, Vol. 20, No. 2, April-June, 1968.

Architects moan about the pitfalls of eclecticism while pointing to the banality of builders' "Cape Cod split-level colonial ranch houses." Criticism at this level is well taken, however the problem lies not in the premise of eclecticism but in its execution. These houses are unattractive not because they assumed the trappings of an "anachronistic historical style," but because the cookie cutter that fashioned them was itself created without skill, taste, or subtlety. It is mainly the younger architects, less inhibited by modernist traditions, who are able to accept a more relaxed view of history. They may be able to use historical forms more freely to create an architecture of their own which is also capable of reflecting its context with sympathy and dignity.

An Aid to Relearning How to Design in Context

The link, or return, has been a panacea for architects, solving all the problems of fitting new buildings to old by allowing us to pretend that the old is no longer there. Once the link is in place, we seem to feel that we can ignore whatever is on the other side.

I suggest that the first thing to do in relearning the skills of designing in context is to exorcise this link from our architectural vocabulary. First solve the purely visual problem of relating *directly* to what is there; the visual cues for the rest of the design should then come more easily from what was learned in making the direct connection.

When designing a free-standing building for an existing context, the visual texture, composed primarily of small scale details (ornament) is usually the critical element. While it is not necessarily recommended, one can ignore many of the theoretically more important design criteria and still succeed by maintaining this visual texture. To understand its constituents, we should study the architectural elements that contribute to its character in the existing context.

Ornament

As ornament is crucial to our interest, it is appropriate to consider certain questions that inevitably come up when ornament is mentioned.

The *cost* of a building is important to both client and architect. Nowadays most of us assume that a building using traditional ornament must be more expensive than one that is modern, that is, which looks simple and sleek and lacks traditional kinds of decoration.

We have been told for decades that modern design is good because it is economical. One apparent reason for this economy was that it banished costly ornament. But it banished only *traditional* ornament; modern architecture has always had its own, often equally expensive version of ornament. It is just that we do not think of it that way because it does not fit the conventional image of decoration. Even now, that term is reserved for embellishments of the traditional, historical variety. It seldom refers to, for example, the miles of function-less, decorative mullions that have been applied to office towers since the 1950's by great "less-is-more-ers" like Mies van der Rohe.* However, when we consider the dictionary definition of ornament—that which adorns—there are any modern details which qualify: dramatic cantilevers which could just as well have been supported by columns; breathtakingly long spans where intermediate columns could have been inserted; large glass areas where masonry or other cheaper materials could have been used; refined jewel-like details like butt-joined, beveled glass and welded stainless steel; exotic materials (the bronze-clad Seagram Building); and perhaps least obvious, the simplicity of modern architecture, which often requires unusual care in workmanship and materials and, unfortunately, particularly attentive maintenance. (The addition to the National Gallery, page 110, is certainly simple and sleek, but its craftsmanship probably cost at least as much, if not more, than that of the addition to the Frick Collection. Cabinetmakers, in fact, were required to do some of the form-work for it, in order to meet the exacting standards of the architect.) Finally, we must remember the ultimate modern ornament, the building whose form is so mannered and sculpture-like that it becomes an ornament itself.

None of these things is, of itself, necessarily bad, ugly or wasteful. The finest modern buildings enrich our lives with exquisite materials and refined details; but they are also more costly with them than they would be without. So, when the problem of relating a new building to a traditional context involves what seems to be an "extra" cost for ornament, whether traditional or modern, remember that, although ornament is seldom itemized in today's budgets, it is rarely omitted in reality. In addition, while any kind of ornament tends to increase cost, people are often more than willing to pay for it.

---

* The Seagram Building has approximately 37,000 linear feet of bronze mullions which have no functional purpose whatsoever.

Town Hall, Munich (1908).

TRADITIONAL ORNAMENT

Traditional and modern ornament are both "extras."

MODERN ORNAMENT

Pittsfield National Bank, Pittsfield, Massachusetts (ca. 1885).
(Credit: Berkshire Eagle.)

ADDED
FLOOR

Pittsfield National Bank after the addition of one more floor,
early in this century. (Credit: David Douillet.)

Appendix A

To the Architects: Some Common Questions About Designing in Context

1. *At what point do you decide to begin "respecting" a given context?*

The first thing is to decide whether or not a given context is worth honoring. This is a decision which should be made jointly by the client, the community, if it is going to be involved, and the architect. Guidelines for this decision should include cultural, heritage, and historical importance, attractiveness, and degree of visual homogeneity.

If it is decided that the existing context is not worth respecting, look to a regional tradition. If this, too, is lacking, then you are on your own. With good fortune later designers will recognize your contribution as a strong focus and respect it when adding their own designs.

If, however, the context is worthy of respect, design to accommodate its visual character, copying or inventing as you like, but always with your overriding concern being the visual consequences of what you are doing. Forget the "honesties" and "integrities" of architecture as we learned them. They were taught by false prophets.

Remember that at all times you are dealing with a specific context. If you come into a neighborhood which you feel is visually coherent—which as yet has few disruptive elements—design a building which closely captures this feeling. Invent if you wish, but do not feel obligated to do so. Do not be afraid to be literal; some of the greatest Western architects have done it.

If you face a transitional situation, where old and new compete to establish a tone and the new does not respect the old, you must choose sides. Pick that which you and the community find most beautiful or most meaningful. If the choice is close, be on the side of the community. They will have to live with it longer than you.

Do not use a bad new building as the starting point just because it is the most recent.

2. *What do you do when the context is not stylistically homogeneous, but a mixture?*

For some years the standard view has been: if the context is not absolutely homogeneous, there is "no context." While this sounds logical—possibly because it is so familiar—the problem is more often that we have simply not been trained to look for the visual continuities in this sort of situation. I do not mean only the obvious kinds of relationships, such as cornice height or similar historical styles, but those which exist between the National Permanent Building and the Old Senate Office Building (page 120), between Quincy Market and its additions (page 122), or between the Park Avenue townhouse and its larger neighbors (page 128). As our eyes are not attuned to these visual relationships we tend to throw up our pencils in despair when presented with a mixture of styles instead of searching out the underlying visual consistencies.

3. When is a radical break with the context appropriate?

In certain situations a violent break with the past is appropriate, even necessary, for its symbolic value. There may be a need to inspire by giving a glimpse of the "future" or by erasing the disagreeable past. This was Prime Minister Nehru's reasoning when, after the partition of India in 1947, he decided to establish the new city of Chandigarh as the capital of the Punjab. The wisdom of such an idea can hardly be questioned given the tragic circumstances of that event. But while the symbolic importance of the gesture is valuable, the need for some manner of cultural and visual continuity should not be underestimated. As it turned out, many of the Western-planned architectural concepts of Chandigarh were ill-chosen for serving the needs of the Indian population. The "future" always has its roots in the present.

The monument—corporate, civic, religious or cultural—can also break with its context without disturbing. But this category, too, has its gray areas. The East Wing of the National Gallery, in Washington, D.C., is a monument. However, it is also the addition to a more important monument (the Gallery itself) which, in turn, is part of the large composition of the Mall.

4. When are less-than-radical increments of change appropriate?

Smaller increments of change happen for many reasons: dilapidation; economic growth; technical obsolescence (the glass box); immigrations; and natural disaster. We may also simply weary of our present surroundings. When they occur, however, it should be noted that they can often be accomplished while still maintaining visual continuity; that is, variety can be achieved while maintaining visual compatibility.

5. Does designing in context necessarily lead to monotony?

There is a difference between a visually coherent context—one in which various buildings are of the same visual character—and a community of total predictability. Modern Rotterdam, built after the war, is monotonous; so are some of the 19th century working class suburbs of London and some Dutch and American suburbs of this century. In these cases, some variety might have been desirable. As with all such questions, it is a matter of taste. I would say that to put a traditional Dutch house in the midst of a boring tract of modern apartments in Rotterdam would almost always be a welcome contrast. To put a bland modern building in the midst of a traditional Dutch street, on the other hand, would almost always be an unmitigated disaster.

There is also a delicate balance between variety which creates lively and visually interesting contrast, and variety which becomes chaotic. Monotony and confusion are but two sides of the same coin and equally unwelcome in a city.

6. How does the idea of sympathetic visual continuity apply at the largest scale of city planning?

Large housing estates, urban renewal areas and whole new towns present a different problem. If there is no immediate architectural context for a new town, there should be, theoretically, few visual restrictions. But be aware of regional styles and what they mean to the larger visual experience. Visual memory is strong and often makes connections over time and space, if you recall our discussion of the Lang House in Connecticut (page 89).

With the exception of new towns, these larger scale planning projects usually do meet existing contexts. They are often large enough to stand alone, and do not necessarily need to be related directly to the context. But their edge conditions should be taken into consideration because they can affect the sense of neighborhood or regional continuity. The range of responses varies depending on whether one is given one lot or three lots to develop, or one city block or sixteen.

Let us assume that we are given six blocks on which to build near the center of a city. What are the choices, assuming that the context is worth respecting?

1) To relate to the existing context throughout the new development.

2) To relate to it only at the edges and to change the visual character, gradually or abruptly, inside its borders.

3) To inject something totally different as a "symbol of the future," the most frequent choice in recent times.

7. *Does maintaining visual continuity in a neighborhood mean there is no possibility for change?*

Of course not. Establishing a sense of visual continuity does not mean embalming a neighborhood. This should be clear from the historical examples. Variety, invention and change are all possible within the bounds of a consistent and coherent visual tradition.

But it has become apparent in recent years that this continuity is most difficult to achieve when designers are tied to an aesthetic which is outspokenly hostile to traditions and which sees a close relationship to the context as a direct threat to creativity.

8. *What about the desire for novelty?*

The desire for novelty is valid. But respecting an architectural context certainly does not preclude the introduction of novelty, even whimsy, into the architectural life of a city. The Dutch street shows this, as have a number of other historical and contemporary examples.

Appendix B

A Handbook for Non-Architects Who Are Concerned About Visual Continuity in Their Communities

This section is intended to help non-architects take advantage of the valuable skills which architects can contribute to their communities. It discusses questions useful to those who want more control over what their neighborhoods look like, particularly when they and their architects have different perceptions about what looks "right" in situations such as the following:

You have been asked to comment on or approve a design presented to your community. The question of relating the proposed building to the existing architectural context has not yet been raised in design reviews but you feel it should be discussed. How do you bring it up?

You are a member of a building committee to whom the architect has presented a design which he or she says DOES fit in well with its surroundings—but your eyes do not believe the architect's words. How can you be specific about your reservations?

You have just learned that a building is going to be built in your community which you feel is inappropriate to its context. No design approvals were required. You have explored alternatives to prevent its being built as is, such as court injunctions, in-

formal community pressure through newspaper articles and community meetings, and formal pressure through local politicians. You need to strengthen your case by stating specific points at which you feel the design fails. How do you identify them?

You, individually, or as a member of a public group, have just hired an architect and want to make it clear from the beginning that you want the building to be sympathetic to its surroundings. The architect asks "What do you mean by 'fitting in'?" How can you be specific?

The Means

There are three important things to do when you are faced with any of these situations:

—You must convey what your criteria are for fitting new architecture with old.

—You must be able to guide the designer so that together you can arrive at a building which fits in to everyone's satisfaction.

—You must be able to evaluate the degree to which the architect's presentation satisfies your criteria.

Conveying the Information

Find buildings, or pictures of buildings, in similar contexts which you feel relate successfully to their surroundings; discuss them with your architect. Remember that, while it is sometimes the easiest way, one need not transfer ideas literally from one situation to another. Some examples in *Architecture In Context* may apply specifically or by analogy to your situation. There may also be examples in your area which help convey the concept of fitting in.

To initiate the dialogue, give the architect a list of questions which you feel raise important issues. Make it clear that you would appreciate having these questions answered explicitly as the design develops. Here are some examples.

1. How will the proposed building relate to its immediate neighbors in terms of such general categories as building set-back, facade proportions, roof silhouette, massing, building material and color?

2. How will the proposed building relate to the visual characteristics of any identifiable historical style in the area?

3. How will the non-historical, small scale ornament of the proposed building relate to the visual characteristics of its immediate neighbors?

As a point of departure for later discussion, show the architect the complete list of evaluative questions at the end of this chapter. Make it clear that you see these as starting points for discussion, not set questions for which there is only one answer. Explain that you understand that just conforming to any ten criteria will not guarantee a good fit-in. You might show examples of buildings in this book which follow the criteria but which still do not establish a successful relationship.

Guiding the Presentation

Request that specific information be given in sketches, presentation drawings and models.

Materials, colors and textures should be clearly shown on drawings. This includes ornament and details *both of the proposed building and the adjacent buildings that will form its context.*

Photographs of the context should be presented with the proposed building superimposed, showing color, materials, textures and details. Drawings could be substituted for photographs but if so, they should all be done by the same hand so that the drawing style is consistent; different styles can convey totally different feelings. Details should not be merely sketched in, on either the existing or the proposed buildings. The drawing style should be realistic.

Sometimes the immediate context is less important than the character of the whole neighborhood or the regional style. In these cases, characteristic examples of the style should be shown. Presentation drawings (or photographs) should also show nearby buildings of exceptional visual importance, even if they are not necessarily seen at the same time as the proposed building.

Samples of existing and proposed materials should be provided when possible, particularly if their color or texture differences are critical.

Architectural models should show materials, colors and textures, along with as much detail as is possible. The white cardboard models now favored often make beautiful objects in their own right but, unless buildings are to be made of white cardboard too, their lack of accurate material and detail indications makes it difficult to judge their impact on the context.

Perspective views of the proposed building should show it as it will be seen by the passer-by. Birdseye perspectives and isometric drawings are sometimes helpful in understanding rudimentary contextual relationships, but can also be misleading. (An "isometric" is a measured drawing that pays some attention to the third dimension but in which the sizes of objects do not diminish as they get farther away, as in perspective.) Isometrics are useful to architects and engineers, but require experience and study to understand. The untrained eye does not readily follow them because they show buildings in ways one never sees them.

Birdseye views are less deceiving, but the best way to understand these relationships is usually by examining a series of perspective views or sketches showing what will actually be seen as you walk by.

Perspectives should include people as well as telephone poles, signs, cars, etc. While some of these are not particularly beautiful, if they are present in reality you should be aware of them in the presentation because they will affect your perception of the final product. (They should not, however, obscure important relationships between the proposed buildings and its neighbors.)

Some examples of presentation techniques which camouflage rather than clarify relationship between new and old architecture are:

Drawings that omit details on adjoining buildings, or which do not show these buildings entirely.

Drawings that hide crucial parts of buildings with trees or landscaping.

Views that show the building from obscure angles.

Evaluating the "Fitness" of a Design

In evaluating how well a proposed building will relate to its context it is essential to remember that this does not depend exclusively on following a rigid set of rules. It may be useful, however, to work from a list of potentially important fit-in characteristics to guide discussions aimed at understanding why a design does NOT fit in, or how to improve a design so that it fits in better.*

An evaluation checklist can be divided into two parts:

1) General Attributes
2) Historical and Non-Historical Style Attributes
The General Attributes will be familiar to many people; most contemporary lists of design criteria contain some or all of these items.

The next category pertains to traditional and

modern ornament. In present-day lists of design criteria, ornament is often mentioned but in practice it receives little attention, as we have seen from the examples. It is assumed that by adapting the design to the General Attributes a successful relationship can be established. The refinement of detail and ornament, however, is one of the surest and easiest ways to make a clear and direct connection between new and old. Small scale ornament can often compensate for quite a broad neglect of the strictures on the General Attributes list by creating a visual character that is especially true to the feeling of the original context.

General Attributes:

Is the proposed building similar or different from its neighbors in:

1. Setback from the street.
2. Spacing from adjoining buildings.
3. Massing: how the main volumes of the building are composed.
4. Approximate height.
5. Facade proportions and directionality.
6. Shape and silhouette.
7. Window and door dispositions.
8. Window and door sizes and proportions.
9. Materials.
10. Color.
11. Scale: how the building is perceived in relation to human size. Is it imperious and intimidating or cozy and friendly? (This is affected by one's expectation of the size of familiar elements like steps, windows and the placement of moldings. See discussion of Nantucket cottages by Venturi & Rauch, page 91.)

Please remember that these are only guidelines! In the preceding examples in this book I have shown perfectly acceptable fit-ins which ignore many of these items; indeed it is conceivable that a designer can ignore all of this list and still produce a successful building. Nevertheless, the rules can be helpful in establishing a relationship, and they can also serve as a checklist to find out why a building just does not "look right" in its setting.

---

* The lists of design criteria from Savannah, Georgia, Sonoma County, California and Lowell, Massachusetts, are particularly good.

Historical and Non-Historical
Style Attributes

At this point we should refer briefly to the discussion of Ornament in the conclusion on pages 144–147. It mentions points which are pertinent to the next two categories.

We next should determine whether the proposed building is similar or different from its neighbors in terms of the specific elements which define *all styles* at the small scale, the character and disposition of its ornament. (See the next category for specific characteristics.)

Ornament Checklist

This final list of questions will help you to determine whether the forms and details of the proposed building clearly capture the *visual feeling* of the existing buildings in terms of the character and disposition of their ornament.

Where does the ornament occur?
At the tops and bottoms of the buildings?
Around windows or doors?
Is it concentrated at focal points, or spread out in a general pattern or texture?
Does it create a feeling of agitation or calm?
Does it create a rhythm? Is it regular or syncopated?
Is color an important ornamental element and if so, how is it used?
Is the dominant feeling of the building, as reinforced by the ornament, one of massive solidity or thinness and linearity?
Is the ornament angular or curving?
Is it soft or hard looking?
Is it visually heavy or light?
Does it look busy or plain?

Discussions between Client and Architect

The foregoing checklists can be useful in isolating problems, generating discussions, and perhaps in resolving the main question: whether or not the differences between new and existing are *visually disturbing*. Does the proposed building stand out because it seems too naked? Too complex? Is the general shape disturbing? Is the siting inappropriate? Or are any or all of these contrasts acceptable?

If the building is disturbing, one should be able to decide where the problems lie by checking through the items on these lists.

The Eye

Architects rarely set out to fool their clients. However, problems arise with conventionally accepted presentation techniques which show off a new design at its best but which may obscure its relationship to the neighboring buildings. Drawing the proposed building with full shadows and detail, while indicating the adjoining ones in line only, obviously highlights the new. And this is, after all, what the architect is trying to sell. But this kind of drawing is not necessarily the best presentation technique for the client who is interested in learning more about the relationship of the proposed building to its future neighbors.

Be wary of verbal descriptions of how well the new fits with the old. Rely first on what your eye tells you and only then on what you are told you are seeing. Phrases like "repeating the proportions of the old windows" may sound right but they are no guarantees of success.

Finally, remember that the quality of the relationship between new and old architecture does not necessarily improve by satisfying more of the criteria on the shopping list. Therefore, rather than relying on checklists when making your final judgment, bring an eye educated to the selection process. Sharpen your ability to make these visual decisions by looking for buildings which you feel do fit in well and asking yourself why they succeed.

And learn to trust your eye.

It may be instructive at this point to mention a recent confrontation—between an architect and his client and the community—in which the community prevailed and the architect had to modify his design.

The location was Old Town Alexandria, Virginia. The project was a proposed courthouse and commercial complex. It was to be a large, modern building, sited among relatively small Georgian and neo-Georgian structures. The architect's problem arose when a number of citizens decided that the proposed building violated the spirit of the neighborhood.

Courthouse and Commercial Building, Alexandria, Virginia; Saunders, Cheng and Appleton (under construction). These are the presentation renderings of the rejected (top) and approved designs (bottom). Although the most pressing question about this design was its relationship to its context, neither rendering showed the proposed design *in* that context. (All details, including such large-scale elements as dormers, were omitted from the presentation model.)

Through newspaper publicity and their very vocal presence at town meetings, these citizens put enough pressure on the design review board to get them to reject the proposal by a narrow 5–4 vote. The revised design is, to the credit of the citizens and the architect, distinctly better suited to its context. Although the architect insisted the buildings' "modern" needs could not be accommodated by a traditional design, the revised version accomplished exactly that. As in earlier examples, it was the ornament which made the bridge; the massing, color and siting of the building remained unchanged. The extra cost amounted to about 2% of the budget. And it was cheap at that, considering what was avoided. (This 2%, by the way, does not take into account deductions such as would occur when the glass-enclosed top floor is replaced with a mansard and dormers; this would yield a probable savings in the cost of materials—if not labor—and a certain savings in long-term heating, cooling and maintenance.)

Ironically, the same architect had already designed several Neo-Georgian buildings for the town. When asked why he had hesitated this time, the response was a muffled "Well, we wanted to do something contemporary."

In the original presentation to the architectural review board the architect justified the design with modernist catch phrases such as "new forms to suit modern needs." This remark assumes that old forms cannot meet new needs. When I asked him directly which version was the more functional, however, he sheepishly admitted that there really was no difference.

This refreshingly frank and perceptive remark was followed by the rather less perceptive comment that the final design was merely "facadism." There was an understandable defensive posture to this statement.

The fact is that much of architecture consists of putting facades on large boxes which have been subdivided into smaller boxes. The style of the facade, in almost every case, is only coincidentally connected to what goes on inside. This is painful for most designers to acknowledge because to do so means relinquishing one of the most potent arguments —"new needs demand new forms"— with which they routinely rationalize their whimsical aesthetic preferences.

Index